What people are

LOVE: EXPRESSED

'Tristan Sherwin has written a smart and beautiful book showing us that Jesus Christ is the love of God expressed as a human life. This is the life we are called to imitate; this life of love is what we are made for. *Love: Expressed* is intensely rooted in Scripture, but drawing upon contemporary culture (film and music, with a smattering of physics), Sherwin's book is comfortably at home in the post-Christendom world of the 21st century.'

Brian Zahnd
Pastor of Word of Life Church, Missouri, USA
and Author of *A Farewell To Mars* and *Beauty will Save the World*

'Refreshing, authentic, inspiring and yet practical, Tristan is a breath of fresh air. His winsome prose and posture as a fellow traveler invites us deeper into the adventure of daily discipleship. Highly recommended'

Jeff Lucas
Author, Speaker, Broadcaster

'I love the personal 'ness' of Tristan's book - I love the provoking 'ness' of it! It reads so easily, and it comforts, yet, draws and probes with challenge! The chapters on obedience and service were highlights in a book I'd love every member of my church to read! A Great Book!'

Victoria Smith-Unwin M.A.
Senior Pastor, Full Gospel Church, New Moston, Manchester, England

'*Love: Expressed* is a book that needs to be out there for all of Christ's followers to read.'

Paul Schofield
Senior Pastor, Metro Christian Centre, Bury, England

LOVE: EXPRESSED

TRISTAN SHERWIN

WESTBOW
P R E S S®
A DIVISION OF THOMAS NELSON
& ZONDERVAN

Scripture quotations taken from the Holy Bible, New Living Translation, Copyright © 1996, 2004. Used by permission of Tyndale House Publishers, Inc., Wheaton, Illinois 60189. All rights reserved.

Scripture taken from THE MESSAGE.
Copyright © by Eugene H. Peterson 1993, 1994, 1995, 1996, 2000, 2001, 2002. Used by permission of NavPress Publishing Group.

Scripture taken from the New King James Version. Copyright © 1979, 1980, 1982 by Thomas Nelson, Inc. Used by permission. All rights reserved.

WestBow Press books may be ordered through booksellers or by contacting:

WestBow Press
A Division of Thomas Nelson & Zondervan
1663 Liberty Drive
Bloomington, IN 47403
www.westbowpress.com
1 (866) 928-1240

Because of the dynamic nature of the Internet, any web addresses or links contained in this book may have changed since publication and may no longer be valid. The views expressed in this work are solely those of the author and do not necessarily reflect the views of the publisher, and the publisher hereby disclaims any responsibility for them.

Any people depicted in stock imagery provided by Thinkstock are models, and such images are being used for illustrative purposes only. Certain stock imagery © Thinkstock.

ISBN: 978-1-5127-1586-6 (sc)
ISBN: 978-1-5127-1587-3 (hc)
ISBN: 978-1-5127-1585-9 (e)

Library of Congress Control Number: 2015917000

Print information available on the last page.

WestBow Press rev. date: 10/23/2015

Dedicated to Steph, Corban and Eaden

CONTENTS

FOREWORD

Tristan Sherwin has written the book about love I feel like I've been looking for, but never found. This is that rare book about love devoid of sentimentality and clichés, that book about theology devoid of jargon and abstractions. *Love: Expressed* is a work of dirt-under-your-fingers spirituality. The love described here is bodily, incarnational, corporeal. You'll know within the first few chapters that the love described here, like the author, is very much *real*.

For my own part, I feel like I've spent so many years trying to get my head around the mystery of what it would mean for us as humans to come to know that we are beloved by God, and what it would mean for us in turn to deeply, robustly love one another. The simplicity of that language is deceitful, in a way: there's nothing in the world harder, even if there is nothing more exhilarating, than living fully awake to love. There is nothing "deeper" than love. There's no way to learn enough about it to somehow graduate on to something else. In the narrative of Scripture, Love is the force behind the entire cosmos. Love is both what created us, and what sustains us. Love is what put us together, and yet if we live long enough we learn that, in the words of Joy Division, "*Love Will Tear Us Apart*". It's the mystery always beneath us—the theoretically simple concept that has to turn us inside out over and over again for us to grasp it, or perhaps for it to grasp us.

What I treasure most about Tristan's book is that it doesn't try to resolve or explain the mysteries of divine or human love, but take us deeper into them.

His clean prose, warmth, wit and pop culture savvy lowered my defenses, and allowed me to feel the shock of full-bodied grace all over again. Step-by-step, then, the word love becomes incarnate here. Love takes on flesh and bone, which is really what the Christian story has always been about. Along the way, some of your old ideas about love will be challenged and deconstructed. But what Tristan offers us in exchange for our hackneyed ways of thinking about love is something more elemental, more primal, more *soulish*...simply put, more true.

When I finished this book, I felt my own soul laid bare, and yet ready all over again to open up my heart, to make myself available to that primal love at the center of things, ever threatening to make me new. It brought to mind a simple, beautiful prayer written by the priest Henri Nouwen. I hope that as you read the pages ahead and let the wonder of divine love seep into you, it can become your prayer too:

"Dear God,
I am so afraid to open my clenched fists!
Who will I be when I have nothing left to hold on to?
Who will I be when I stand before you with empty hands?
Please help me to gradually open my hands
and to discover that I am not what I own,
but what you want to give me.
And what you want to give me is love,
unconditional, everlasting love.
Amen."[1]

--*Jonathan Martin*
Author of *Prototype*

INTRODUCTION: **AXIS**

'We look forward to the time when the Power
of Love will replace the Love of Power. Then will
our world know the blessings of peace.'
William Gladstone[1]

'JE SUIS' FLESH – THE DIVINE CRITIQUE

Have you ever seen the film *Kill Bill Vol. 2* by Quentin Tarantino?

Yes, you *are* looking at a book about love, and I understand that referencing to that film might not appear to line up with its context.

But I'll be honest with you; I need a starting point, something that will make you wonder, something that will raise your curiosity. So I'm choosing that starting point to be Tarantino.

You see, I love the way that Q.T. writes dialogues and monologues within his films; my all-time favourite piece of monologue coming from the film just mentioned. It's near the end of the movie, as the title character Bill, played by *David Carradine*, starts discussing the uniqueness of *Superman's* alter ego in contrast to the other heroes of the comic book universe.

As Bill points out, most of the other heroes, like *Peter Parker* and *Bruce Wayne*, weren't born super; they had to *become* super. Something had to happen to them in order to project them into their journeys as *Spider-Man* and *Batman* – either some freak science experiment or the manifestation of an acute psychological childhood trauma – and both of them had pretty steep learning curves in discovering what they had become and what they were capable of. But *Superman*, well, he crash-landed here as *Superman*. He didn't have to learn to be super; as he grew up, he had to learn to be human. He didn't have to learn to develop his abilities; he had to learn to hide and repress them. *Superman* never transformed into *Superman*, there's no origin story about how he got his powers; his genesis is really about how he becomes Clark Kent. Clark Kent is to *Superman*, what the black mask, the shadows and the body armour are to *Bruce Wayne*; a disguise to protect his real identity. *Spider-Man* wears a latex red and black-webbed mask, but the *Man of Steel's* costume isn't the blue suit with the red cape and the matching underpants; it's the pair of thick-rimmed glasses and the cheap-looking suit. *Superman's* outfit is actually in the form of a clumsy newspaper reporter.

It's at this point, when you begin to see Clark Kent as camouflage, that Tarantino's movie monologue begins to hit its climax; as Bill sharply points out that Kent is *Superman's* attempt to appear and to act as human as possible, it's his presentation of how he perceives us. And how does he perceive us? What traits does Clark display in order to remain incognito? In Bill's description: Kent is 'weak', he lacks confidence, and he's a 'coward'. That, according to Bill, is how *Superman* manages to resemble all of us; it's this Kryptonian's evaluation of what it is to be a human being.[2]

'A critique of humanity' – I find that a fascinating way to think about *Superman's* alter-ego; that the *Man of Steel's* false persona as the 'mild-mannered' reporter for the *Daily Planet* was just his modelled expression of his assessment on the human condition. Could it be that when we look at Kent, we're given this outsider's opinion of what it means to be flesh? If so, then it's almost like he's mocking us in a way that says: 'I can be like you, but you can never be like me'.

Which is a shame, because wouldn't we want to become like *Superman* – excluding the obvious embarrassment of wearing underpants on the outside of your trousers?

I remember being a child, fastening my jacket around my neck as a makeshift cloak and running around the school playground with one arm raised above my head to simulate flying. I would jump to indicate when I was taking off. I would jump again and crouch slightly to show that I had landed and then slowly rise, with my hands resting on my hips and my elbows pointing outward – you had to have the hero stance! In my imagination, I was rescuing damsels, saving the world and attempting to bring order to the chaos.

So I have to be real with you – if someone, tomorrow, offered us a single injection that would give us the same abilities as *Superman* (minus the x-ray vision, because I'm not certain we could be trusted with that), then I'd be extremely tempted to say, 'Yes'.

Wouldn't most of us take it? And I'm certain that many of us would accept that injection with the right motives; we'd hope that in possessing those great powers we would also possess the abilities to transform our world for the better.

Which is revealing, isn't it?

Because deep down, in our admission to this want, aren't we then also subconsciously agreeing with Bill's perception of *Superman's* critique of our flesh-life condition? Does *Superman's* expression through Clark Kent maybe confirm our paranoia that the human condition is weak, impotent and ill-equipped to make the world a better place?

We want to be like *him* because we feel that being like *us* isn't enough.

But what if our humanity is a gift and not a curse? What if we already possess the means to change the world for the better? And what if those means aren't located in being able to fly or in some mighty latent strength within our muscles, but within our capacity to love?

What if *The Beatles* were right, and love really is all that is needed?

I believe Jesus gives us a better critique of the human condition than *Superman*; a divine critique. A critique that, on the one hand, does point out our failings, weaknesses and our lack of courage, but at the same time also gives us hope; hope that the reality we seek isn't to be found in some power-giving injection, but in the lived-out expression of what it really means to be human, to live as an image bearer of the divine.

Of course, some of my friends and work colleagues will accuse me of jumping from one fictional comic book character to another more ancient one at this point. And we could – if I possessed the ability – go into some historical detour in an attempt to demonstrate whether the Jesus we read about within the pages of the New Testament ever existed or not. But I'm not going to do that here, as doing so would move us away from the purpose of this book[3]. However, if we seriously considered what the early followers of Jesus believed and declared about Him, and what Jesus said about Himself, then we are presented with an extraordinary reality: that Jesus is God in flesh...

... God *became* like us.

The creator, an outsider, came and made his home with us; walked with us; talked with us; ate with us; wept with us; laughed with us; died like us.

As one writer within the New Testament puts it:

'For in Christ the fullness of God lives in a human body...'[4]

And yet within that manifestation, even though He does do some rather extraordinary things like walking on water and turning water into wine, we don't see Jesus flying at the speed of light around the world in order to reverse time, nor do we read of Him shooting laser beams from his eyes. In fact, most of the time, He's pretty normal-looking in both

His appearance and His behaviour. He's human. I have to mention this, and not in any way to demean God's greatness, but Jesus isn't God's alter ego, like Clark Kent is to Superman. Jesus is fully God, and yet fully human. He's not merely God disguised as a man, but a manifestation of God.

I love this, and I appreciate that the subtlety of this might not be obvious, but God didn't seem to mind being made of skin and bones. And actually, if we think about it, and when we look at His life amongst us, He does an awful lot through what we would consider a restraint to our capacity.

We would believe that we need to be more than human to transform our world. But God, through the incarnation, enters into creation. He embodies it. He embraces it. He enjoys it. And through it He expresses, not only who He is, but also what humanity is called to be. As one of my favourite authors puts it, *'Clearly God does not feel limited by the human canvas'*[5].

Where *Superman* comes and shows us what we can never be, God comes and shows us what we are called to be.

In Jesus, we are given a clear picture of what the partnership between human and divine is supposed to look like. In Jesus, God enters creation and displays its potential. In Jesus, we are shown a human life lived in all its fullness. In Jesus, we are given the physical demonstration of the early church's motif that 'God is love'...

... Jesus is love: expressed.

Please understand, this isn't going to be a book about performing miracles. I don't know whether you've ever seen a supernatural miracle or not. I don't know whether you'll participate in something like raising the dead, or healing a blind man or anything else that is naturally beyond our human capacity. But I know this: that we are all capable of love, and that it is only love, a divine love expressed through a divine image, that can change the world.

More than this, I believe that this love has already come amongst us and has already changed the world, and continues to change this world. How this has happened, and how this continues to happen, is part of the substance of this book – but not the only part.

THE MOST IMPORTANT THING

There's a story within the New Testament, a moment where Jesus finds Himself faced with a question from a member of the crowd that had gathered to hear Him speak. The question went something like this: 'Of all the commandments, which is the most important?'[6].

The word *commandment* might seem a little outdated for most of us, and I suppose in modern terms it could be reworded in numerous ways, but I'm going to rephrase it as follows:

'What's the most important thing that I can do with my humanity?'

Jesus' response to this question is world famous – and will pop up again later in this book. He replies;

'"...You must love the Lord your God, with all your heart, all your soul, all your mind, and all your strength". The second is equally important: "Love your neighbour as yourself". No other commandment is greater than these.'[7]

Jesus says the most important thing is love. And interestingly, Jesus seems to struggle in being able to separate loving God from also loving those around us.

But I have to ask, do we agree with Jesus' answer? And the answer to that question can't be given with a simple 'yes' or 'no' response; it can only be given by examining the trajectory of our lives.

Maybe there are those who would disagree? Maybe for some of us, we feel the best pursuit of our time, the best investment of our existence would be in the pursuit of power, fame and fortune. Again, like with the

Superman-Injection, we may pursue those things with good motives, assuring ourselves that if we could attain the influence that comes with them, then maybe we could impact the world for the better. And I wouldn't necessarily disagree; there certainly exist people who have these things and who have done so.

But why not pursue love?

Why do we feel suspicious about love's ability to change the world?

Why do we doubt its potential and potency?

Why is it that even holding a book with the word *love* written on the front cover makes us uneasy, especially when in public?

I'm going to hazard a guess at this point – I guess you were initially suspicious of this book when you picked it up? Maybe, as you read the title, you pulled the same face that some of my friends did when I told them the book's topic (and by the way, some of those faces belonged to Christians).

To be brutally honest, maybe the only reason you've made it this far is because I didn't start by talking about love, but about *Tarantino*? As strange as it may sound, I knew that talking about love would potentially put you off (like I said, I needed a starting point).

And who could blame you for being put off. We've heard people talk about love before and we've been amused by its apparent failure. To echo the meaning of a few words from Jon Bon Jovi's *Blaze of Glory*; we feel that love just gets slaughtered in the crossfire as it feebly attempts to bring about real lasting change[8]. And what could be a more reinforcing symbol of love's failure – in the minds of some – than the man who talked about love, hanging naked, scourged and bloody on a cross? For these people, connecting Jesus' death with the idea of love winning just seems like a contradiction in terms.

Could it be though, that we're put off love because we actually have the wrong idea of love?

In our modern, western culture the idea of love has been hijacked to describe everything from sex to sloppy sentimentality. So it's hard to talk about *it* without one of those two extremes influencing our thoughts. To some people – maybe a lot of people – because love has become tethered so closely with attraction and emotions, it has become neither attractive nor emotive. We've reduced love to a feeling, and to help us in doing so – in order for us to reinforce the idea that love is just a myth – we've bought into all the scientific rhetoric that declares that all feelings are nothing more than just potent reactions of our brain's chemical mixtures.

But love isn't a feeling; it is a commitment of the will.

To be clear here, the above isn't a critique of secular culture alone, it also includes the church. As I said before, some of those who pulled a face when I told them of this book's topic were followers of Jesus, and their face said it all: 'Really?' If I'd written a book about leadership, or on achieving your dreams, they may have been more intrigued. But pursuing love wasn't something that sparked their interest.

I want to give a diagnosis here, and I don't want to sound cynical, but I understand that it's difficult not to be taken that way when I say this; some parts of the community that claim to follow God's expression of love, are sick of love.

In some areas of the church we seldom talk about love. Like the secular society around us, we talk more about having influence and vision. We long to create leaders, but not lovers. And although some may defend their stance by stating that love must be part of the 'make up' of a leader, my problem is still the same – love seems to take a secondary position to influence; it's part, but not the whole; it's veneer, but not substrate. Shouldn't this be the other way round? Shouldn't great lovers, those who are prepared to lay down their lives, make the best leaders (better phrased, servants)?

We promote the importance of vision; how a clear vision unites people. But again, to risk sounding cynical, although I agree with the need for vision in our lives, it's important to note that vision causes as much division as it does unity. And could it be that love is the only thing that can overcome this division? It's revealing that in most of the church leader conferences I've attended – especially those that have stressed the importance of Jesus' prayer for unity in John 17 – have often taught that the key ingredient of 'being one' is to have a great vision, whereas Jesus roots the words of His prayer within the love relationship He has with the Father.

For Jesus the most important thing was love. It was the most important commandment of the Old Testament community and it's the founding law of the New Testament community; we are to replicate His love[9]. And expressing the love of God should define us and move us in a way that is counter-cultural to those seeking fame and fortune. As Brian Zahnd points out, about the calling of the church:

> *'We are from the Future. In a world motivated by the primal lusts for money, sex, and power, we are to be a prophetic witness of a future motivated by love. We reject greed, immorality, and domination, not so much because they are "against the rules", but because the future belongs to love. The masters of suspicion are most suspicious of love. Marx says it's all about money. Freud says it's all about sex. Nietzsche says it's all about power. All three ultimately reject the validity of love. But we are to prove the masters of suspicion wrong. Jesus says it's all about love – and we are called to prove that Jesus is right! We do it by living here and now as a people motivated, not by money, sex, and power, but by love.'* [10]

Surely the biggest vision and influence we can ever desire for our lives is to have the capacity to love just as God loved us?

But Jesus' words, about loving God and loving people, still puzzle me.

Because, how is that meant to look exactly?

ORIENTEERING

Which brings us to the other part of this book; I want to explore this question: How does it look to love God and to love people?

Now please don't panic.

Yes, this is a book about love. But this isn't going to become about romance, or feelings, or marriage, or sex… This isn't going to be a plea to become a 'hugger' or to have a bit more of a skip in your step as you walk down the street. And for those who have a phobia of word-studies; this isn't going to be an exploration into the different Greek words for love and their meanings (*philo*, *eros*, a*gape* etc…).

It may also help to say that this isn't a further attempt to be yet another (and unwanted) exposition of that famous '*Love is…*' passage within the New Testament. I've purposely avoided that passage within this book (with the obvious exception of here, of course). It's not that I dislike it – personally, I think it's a great passage – but some of us have grown used to reading and hearing those familiar phrases as if they only belong within things like greeting cards, which isn't where their author intended them to be written[11].

But maybe I've got you wrong; maybe you weren't panicking about this becoming a *Mills & Boon* version of the Jesus story, or troubled about this becoming a collection of agony aunt material?

Maybe what worried you was the word 'How'?

So let me be clear on what is about to follow; what follows is not some attempt to create a creed or establish rules.

I appreciate the risk here; some might see this book as such and misunderstand it as a set of lessons on morality, lessons that seek to provide us with *the* criteria to help us with distinguishing who's really *in* and who's actually *out*.

But that isn't the case at all.

I'm not attempting to moralise – and I hope I have succeeded in not doing so – I'm simply trying to orientate.

In taking Jesus as our axis, can we examine how He loved, to enable and encourage us to replicate that love?

I hope that you will continue reading this and that, somewhere within each chapter, you'll discover things that would both bless and inspire you. I hope that this love which we explore together would also shock you, disturb you, and maybe even make you rethink and change the orientation of some of the things that you already do.

But *please* don't confuse this with a book on standards or rules.

When we think 'rules' we begin to worry about our ability to follow them, and what it means for us when we don't. Suddenly our focus shifts from expression to performance, which is a dangerous change in our orientation towards the love expressed to us through Jesus.

And so with that in mind, I feel that it's important as we begin this journey to first explore the expression of love known as *obedience*.

'You are Christ's body – that's who you are! You must never forget this. Only as you accept your part of that body does your "part" mean anything... And yet some of you keep competing for so-called "important" parts. But now I want to lay out a far better way for you'
– 1 Corinthians 12:27-31 (The Message)

PROLOGUE: **THE POOL**

Afterward Jesus returned to **Jerusalem** for one of the Jewish holy days. Inside the city, near the Sheep Gate, was the pool of **Bethesda**, with five covered porches. **Crowds** of sick people—blind, lame, or paralyzed—lay on the porches, **[waiting for a certain movement of the water**, for an angel of the Lord came from time to time and stirred up the water. And the first person to step in after the water was stirred was healed of whatever disease he had]. One of the men lying there had been sick for thirty-eight years. When **Jesus saw** him **and** knew he had been ill for a long time, he **asked** him, *"Would you like to get well?"*

*"***I can't***, sir,"* the sick man said, *"for I have no one to put me into the pool when the water bubbles up. Someone else always gets there ahead of me."*

Jesus told him, *"***Stand up***, pick up your mat, and walk!"*

Instantly, the man was **healed**! He rolled up his sleeping mat and began walking! **But** this miracle **happened on the Sabbath**, so the Jewish **leaders objected**. They said to the man who was cured, "You can't work on the Sabbath! **The law doesn't allow** you to carry that sleeping mat!"

But he replied, "The man who healed me told me, 'Pick up your mat and walk.'"

"Who said such a thing as that?" they demanded.

The man didn't know, for Jesus had disappeared into the crowd. But **afterward Jesus found him** in the **Temple** and told him, "Now you are well; so stop sinning, or something even worse may happen to you." Then **the man went and told the Jewish leaders that it was Jesus** who had healed him.

- John 5:1-15 (NLT)

EXPRESSED THROUGH **OBEDIENCE**

'Our surrender doesn't produce God's favour;
God's favour produces our surrender'
Tullian Tchividjian[1]

WARNING

A part of me doesn't want to write this chapter. The whole topic makes me nervous, nervous because of the understandings and baggage that come with the word *obedience*. I'm aware that even before getting to this chapter, the likelihood is that you saw its title on the contents page and your mind instantly filled with ideas, experiences, stories and expectations about what this chapter might have to say on the subject. I hazard a guess that most of the stuff filling your mind when you saw the word *obedience* was negative – it's the same in my mind also. I'm sure that between the two of us, it wouldn't take long to brainstorm some of the abuses, atrocities and injustices that have been inflicted and demanded as acts of submission.

If this wasn't enough to contend with, I'm also aware that the contents of this book will be viewed as 'religious' or 'spiritual', with the possibility of it being labelled 'Christian Life' on the back cover, giving it all the hallmarks of being yet another kind of instruction manual on 'how to do life for God'. Sadly this doesn't begin to counterbalance the influx of negative brainwaves. And then, to top it all, I have weaved the

1

word *love* into the subject matter, it's all over the front cover and the synopsis on the back. With the combination of *love* and *obedience* our minds can begin to suspect that somewhere, lying in wait within the paragraphs to come, is an ambush of guilt to coax us into doing things we have no desire to do as a proof of our devotion.

So first I must apologise and ask your forgiveness, because my purpose within the pages that follow is not to deal with all the baggage surrounding obedience by denouncing this or that. Time and space within this chapter does not allow us to take a few events from our histories and turn them over in an attempt to place them within moral categories. But I do hope that what I say adds to and enriches the dialogue of what it means to be obedient.

I would also like to give some caution about how we should proceed – If your hope right now, as you enter this chapter, is to find biblical examples, stories or illustrations, that you feel will aid you in demonstrating to someone else why they need to submit to your authority, then please follow my advice; close this book, put it down, walk away and spend some time in conversation with God.

The pages that follow are not about the demanding of obedience from people, but about the display of devotion towards God and others. Love, in its very essence, is expression not extraction, so this chapter is not about gaining the control of anyone or anything, but about relinquishing it. And actually, maybe our urge to control isn't a bad place to start.

CONTROL FREAKS

I have a major weakness: *chocolate* – so much so, that I almost want to re-type that word using a capital C! Just one look at a bar of chocolate sends my senses into automatic recall, making the smooth textures and creamy tastes of all my previous (and numerous) liaisons come rushing back. So, because of this cocoa induced daydream, I will often find myself failing to reject the advances of a vending machine.

It's their transparency that's my downfall – it would be easier to say 'no' if only pictures of chocolate bars were to be found on the front of the machine, but that wouldn't bring in many sales. No, through their acrylic windows, vending machines unashamedly declare, 'Here sits what could be yours'. An image is easy to resist, but with the actual thing it's not so simple – especially when I know that all it takes to have my desires dispensed is to meet the machine's demands by pressing the right buttons and exchanging the required amount.

Except sometimes it's not that straightforward, is it?

I've often found myself bowing in humility to collect my money, along with my broken dreams, from the machine's rejection bin – all because the system's hyper-sensitivity detected something wrong with my offering. Ironically, this always seems to happen when I only have the one coin to offer. But I want *my* Chocolate, so what do I do? I try again, and again... and again. Sometimes, the machine responds to such faithful persistence, but now and then I have to try a little harder to persuade it to swallow what I have to give. This has happened so often throughout the years, that I have developed and gleaned a 'very particular set of skills' for situations such as these.[2]

There are two 'persuasive' tactics that I begin with. The first is to place some *spin* on the coin as I push it into a machine. This spinning motion, as the coin descends, causes it to ricochet off the insides of the machine and hopefully rebound into the 'acceptable' hole (well, at least that's what I imagine takes place). My thinking is that sometimes it's not enough to merely 'drop' a coin into a slot – sometimes, it has to fall with style.

My other primary counter is *friction* – which involves rubbing a coin frantically between the palms of my hands, or on the side of my trousers, in the hope that the static charge infused into the coin will make it more attractive to the fickle tastes of the machine.

And you can't just try these once! No, I will find myself swapping between both approaches at least three times – sometimes even combining the two together. This is how it is with mechanical systems;

being persuasive often seems to be a combination of finding the correct etiquette and being persistent in that pursuit.

And if neither of these approaches work? Then I employ the 'game changer'. Because I have no idea where any coin has been, or whether it's ever been used in such tactical strikes before, this has to be the final move before I have to swallow the hard truth that my coin is a phoney – I pop the coin in my mouth. Not for too long, but long enough to allow the coin to have a good coating of my saliva. Desperate times... etc. The concept is simple enough; the stickiness slows the coin's velocity, giving it more time to be 'chosen' (although, when success does come, it's probably because the gunk on the coin has been washed off).

Although all of these operations seem different, they all share the same motive: *I am trying to discover an acceptable action that will provoke the machine to give me the response I want.*

Unfortunately, this is how many of us understand cause and effect. Though wrong, there is this expectation of life that 'the right action in equals our desired response out'. Whether it's to society's rules, our own rules, a company's rules, a friend's rules, or a deity's rules – it's easy to delude ourselves into believing that our 'obedience' to something is the acceptable currency of transaction into the vending machine picture we sometimes hold of life.

This delusion is highlighted by the frustration we feel when the machine just doesn't play along. Regardless of the differences in our belief/non-belief systems, we are all shocked when bad things happen to us, and we are equally surprised when extraordinarily good things happen to us. Both prompt the 'how' question that arises when we sense a disconnection between our input and the circumstances that surround us.

Even within religion, or should I say especially within religion, we can act in the hope that our obedience to a set of regulations and rituals will provide us with a level of control over life; over our environment, our circumstances, and maybe even over God. We feel that if we do this and not that, pray at the right times and in the right ways, then things will work out for us. We do life with the expectation that our movements will cause life to march ultimately to our will as we dance to the tune of someone else's. Overall then, our obedience isn't about submission, but manipulation.

Instead of doing good because it is the right thing to do, we do it in the hope of keeping ill health away.

Instead of praying to enjoy God and develop our relationship with him, we pray to keep our attendance record looking good – confident that doing so will ward off punishments and keep our ideas of blessings flowing.

Instead of giving financially because we are passionate about a cause, we hand over cash like it's some kind of payment protection scheme – which makes God look like some kind of insurance broker or mafia boss (I wanted to say 'God-Father', but I was afraid some people might be confused with the point I'm making).

It's important that we expose this way of thinking, because if we're not careful, our obedience comes into being not as an expression of love, but as an act of fear.

What pains me most is that there are 'religious' people out there who manipulate others with these very ways of thinking; teaching that health, wealth, plus whatever else you desire will be yours if you 'simply' hand over X amount of money, or if all you do is follow these ten steps etc. I don't accept this as the Good News of Jesus. I don't believe that the gospel reinforces the picture of a 'vending machine' control over life – I believe it actually shatters it to pieces. Jesus doesn't say take a grip of your life, but he calls us to let it go[3].

Why do read your bible? Why do you volunteer? Why do you go to church? Why do you lead a church? Why do you *continue* to lead a church? Is it motivated by love or is it just spiritual OCD?

You see, when obedience to God is lived with this kind of control mentality, being a follower of Christ becomes no more than superstition with a decorative, and maybe more socially acceptable, disguise. Jesus' name, and everything that we claim to do in that name, becomes nothing more than the saliva-covered coin that we hope the system will find pleasing.

This thinking is regularly confirmed by encounters with people who have given up one kind of religion, or 'way' of life, in exchange for another, all because *it* 'didn't work for them'. I've met people who have come to Jesus, and stopped following Jesus, for that very same reason. Dare I admit it – there are times when I have felt like walking away from Jesus because he 'didn't work for me'. In such cases I have to really question whether *Conversion* has actually taken place, instead of just simple *Transference*. Did I come to Jesus, because I recognised him as '*The* Way... etc. or just *another* way of making life swallow my currency?

But what if our actions didn't control as much as we thought?

Don't misunderstand me, rules are important and breaking them can cause an awful lot of pain and mess. Don't think you can turn in late every day to work and not get fired or disciplined. Don't think that you can drive at 70mph on the wrong side of the road and not cause a major catastrophe. But at the same time, let's not be fooled into thinking that arriving on time to work every day, or following every clause within the Highway Code, will guarantee that you will never lose your job or ever be involved in a car accident[4].

Please hear me here, this isn't an argument against doing good or a protest against any sort of 'social contract' or 'Moral Law', this is about resetting our thinking on *why* we practise obedience.

What if our actions today are impotent to provide any guarantee to the positives we hope tomorrow is pregnant with?

We all bring our particular set of skills, playing the system – but what if the call to follow Jesus is a call to escape the machine and to abandon our vain attempts to manipulate it?

WAITING FOR MOVEMENT

It must have been a picture – the pool of Bethesda mentioned by the writer of the fourth Gospel, as described in John chapter 5. A pool of water, mainly stagnant, surrounded by five covered porches, under which sat crowds (John's words, not mine) of sick people – blind, lame, paralysed. All of them are waiting for one thing; 'a certain movement of the water' – this would be the voice that would call all nearby to abandon their comfort and plunge towards the surface. If they were fortunate enough to be the first to enter, then they would be the one to arise healed and free.

John's Gospel doesn't tell us if this happened to be true or not, whether John believed it credible or just false hope – did this pool actually heal people? All John is telling us is that those who gathered there believed it was so. This was their system. All they had to do was make an acceptable entrance into this vending machine of liquid and then their desired response would be dispensed. So there they would sit, waiting and watching for the pool's command which would signal when their obedience should begin.

This is an odd place.

It's called Bethesda – which means 'house of grace' – but this is anything but. Nothing is dispensed for free in this place. As the man's words in John 5:7 show us, help and love were not the ethos of the community that lay under these porches. If anything, this was more like a house of competition. Can you imagine for one moment, the response of this crowd when that 'certain movement' came? How many would be crushed, pushed and hurt by the stampede of people heading towards the water's edge? One person would leave healed (maybe?), but how many more would be left in a worse condition than when they first arrived? How many would drown?

And another thing; 'a certain movement'! It's not the best description to give – what did this movement actually look like? Was it some bubbling up? Was it a ripple going from the east side of the pool to the west? Did you have to get into the water the very second the movement occurred, or could you wait thirty seconds before the healing properties dispersed thoroughly? Did your entrance have to be graceful and elegant, or were you allowed to dive-bomb?

Would you really take the risk in getting it wrong?

I hazard a guess that opinion of this movement would have been divided within the crowd. I imagine a place where different schools of theology had developed, with those of shared conviction gathering together – each denomination holding as sacred a particular style of movement. With every failed healing, every failed attempt to reach the water and every bad entry, not only amplifying these theological divisions, but also serving to reinforce the mystical properties of this water; only *perfect* obedience to its demands would provide the results one sought.

Everyone here is an expert at classifying ripples, or at the very least an expert in training, but none of them have actually experienced the thing that they specialise in.

This place, that is meant to bring people freedom, actually ends up leading people into captivity. When John describes the occupants as 'blind, lame, paralysed', I can't help but feel – with every reading of the story – that their conditions have transcended from physical to spiritual. None can afford to take their eyes off the water before them, none can afford to look at the conditions of those around them who share their prison, no one can afford to help anybody else, and no one can afford to miss their 'divine calling'. No one even has the courage to raise a voice and offer the suggestion – 'Hey, why don't we all get in and just wait?' (And, if that suggestion seems ridiculous to you, then you've just reinforced my point!)

They are a lost people, trapped within a mechanical system of fear and control – a system that requires broken people to save themselves, using abilities they do not possess. This pool asks, but it gives no answers. This pool calls, but it offers no help. This pool demands obedience, but only highlights the failures of those who attempt to meet its rules. This pool uses the hope of acceptance to entice those in need, but only reinforces their feeling of rejection. It almost sounds like a Greek tragedy.

But here they sit, all waiting for movement – all waiting for the right wave to come along.

Does this sound familiar? In seeing this scene, maybe our minds begin to make a connection with organised religion, but the concept is sown into all our patterns of living. Such an idea should hardly survive within our twenty-first century society, but this same mindset is everywhere. We are drowning in a world full of 'isms'; we are all living in obedience to the fluid motion of some pond.

Most of the people I have met (myself included), have found themselves waiting for a wave. Maybe our system isn't a spiritual one, or one that revolves around a deity, but our lives still keep watch on the waters of life, waiting for the prompts and ripples – the signals that will summon our obedience. Our language about our futures is consistently filled with talk of *When* and *Then*. 'If I can be in the right place, at the right time, and produce the right action, then life will dispense my desires'.

And we all have desires – most of which boil down to wanting that elusive/ambiguous/mysterious thing called 'happiness'. We crave meaning, value, purpose and function. We long to live. And so we're happy to keep spinning our saliva-coated offering into whatever system we think will guarantee that.

We place our hopes in our own ability to respond acceptably to life's unpredictable movements. Such thinking places us as the captain of our own vessel, charting the currents, and navigating the deep waters. We feel this false sense of control, that we are the masters, when in reality we are slaves to the water's allure.

It's into this mechanical system, this fluid vending machine, where Jesus enters and totally messes with our thinking.

USURPING GRACE

'*Would you like to get well?*' This is Jesus' question to a man who has been sick for thirty-eight years, and who's spent ample time staring at the waters. Each time I read this I often think 'well, yeah, duh!' Who around this pool didn't want to get well? Surely the man's attendance clearly signified his desire for wholeness. It seems such an insensitive question – imagine asking this to someone on a hospital ward.

But there's something deeper here, there always is when Jesus asks questions.

Imagine for a moment that you were this man and this question was asked of you – how would you respond?

This feels like such a shameful thing to admit, but it took me more than a few attempts to pass my driving test. After receiving my first results, I remember thinking 'not everyone passes first time'. I encouraged myself with thoughts that not all the best drivers passed on their first exam. Actually, most of the people I didn't like getting into a car with – the really crazy drivers – passed first time, so maybe it was a good thing that I failed to notice the unmarked junction? Despite the failure, I felt confident when approaching the second test. However, approaching the fifth driving exam was demoralising.

What made it worse was that a few people I worked with at the time had asked me whether I actually wanted to drive! That hurt. Could they not see how much effort I was putting in? Did they just think I enjoyed failure? Why else would I continue throwing finance at this? Why else would I allow myself to face further embarrassment?

If I was this 'pool-gazing hopeful' I would envisage my answer to Jesus being a defensive rant similar to the one that I spouted towards my work colleagues. A rant filled with all the things that I had done, the sacrifices I had made, an offering up of the evidence that I had given everything I had to this cause. My tone would be filled with shock and injury that I had even been asked such a question – 'How dare you! Can't you see my dedication?'

But this man's response is different.

He doesn't begin to pull out his medals of faithfulness and unwavering commitment to this so-called divine movement. He doesn't mention anything about the amount of time or loss of earnings he has sacrificed to be here instead of begging at some roadside. His reply is short. Only pointing to the brokenness of himself and the system he is trapped within, his answer is filled with an acceptance of his inability and his need for help.

'I can't'.

It's into this offering that Jesus pours His power.

The pool only helps those who help themselves, but Jesus responds to this man's helplessness. Producing a reaction that cannot be generated by the man's activity – or lack of it – and usurping the water's rigorous quality controls, Jesus dispenses healing.

Suddenly Jesus' words have become the currency of change, but they are not spoken into the man's environment, or circumstances, but into the very nature of the man himself.

It's important to see that this man's actions have carried no value in this transaction, his previous life of morality/immorality and theological viewpoint are not even raised – he doesn't even know Jesus' name! Jesus just pours out His life and power, not because He is being controlled nor manipulated by the man's obedience, it's just because He wants to. It's simply *grace*.

This seems unjust, doesn't it? It plays against our understanding of the mechanics of the machine – this man has done nothing to receive such output. What he obtains is outside of the system's movements and protocol. But this is the usurping nature of grace. And it is this same grace that Jesus shows towards us; our actions have not been counted, regardless of whether they were obedient or disobedient. It's Jesus' righteousness, his right actions, which have made all the difference. As Paul writes in Philippians 3:9 –

'I no longer count on my own goodness or my own ability to obey God's law, but I trust Christ to save me' (NLT)

You may be thinking, 'How have we ended up talking about grace, when we were talking about obedience?' But it's important that we don't disconnect the two. A conversation about obedience without the recognition of what Jesus has done quickly becomes a conversation about legalism. Grace is the starting point and the context of our expression of love towards God. It's by God's grace that we have been rescued, and it's His grace *alone* that keeps us that way.

But let's just pause for a second.

I'm conscious that even at this point we might be developing another way to play the system – we might be looking at this man's example and developing another tactic of manipulation. Maybe we're thinking that we can add this man's approach, his confession, his inability to our growing list of methodologies to get what *we* want; adding it to our repertoire of skills which already includes our own versions of 'Spin', 'Friction' and 'Stickiness'. After all, the man got what he desired – healing. But, that would be missing the point in this story. Again, Jesus wasn't coaxed into doing this, he doesn't respond to this man's obedience/faithfulness – he didn't even respond to this man's faith in Him, as the man didn't show any. Jesus responded to this man's need of something that transcended the system – Himself.

We have the same need. If we took the time to really explore our desires – the things that we are desperately seeking, the hopes that keep us mesmerized to the water's movements – we would soon see that He is all that we have ever wanted.

And to be clear here, when I say that we have *need* of Jesus, I don't mean as some crutch – that would just be making Him another means to *our* ends. Through my short years as a follower of Jesus, He has helped me, and is still helping me to see that He is not the means to me attaining or avoiding things that pertain to my description of life – He is Life, in all its fullness.

I need to mention this, it's important that we grasp what this means right at the outset of this book; the life of someone who trusts in Jesus is not about us transferring our hopes onto Jesus, treating Him like an alternative to a rabbit's foot or a zodiac reading. This is about our hopes converging onto and converting into Jesus.

We need to realise that what the 'systems' advertise to us through their transparent acrylic/liquid window is not actually satisfying us. We *need* more than just a dip in some stagnant pond which is occasionally fed by the trickle of an underground stream and masquerades itself as grace (Bethesda) – we need a baptism in living water. *Real* life doesn't come from a system, whether that's a religious one or a secular one; true life comes from God alone, and the life He offers cannot be earned, it can only be received.

Jesus calls us away from the places like Bethesda – places where, at best, all we ever receive is a distorted reflection of ourselves as we helplessly watch the movements of the surface – and calls us to Himself.

This all starts with the expression of *His* love, by *His* grace, so that we can receive *Him*.

The call is not to performance, but to expression. Following Jesus, being obedient to Him, is not about the activity of our lives becoming constant attempts to catch divine ripples by being in the right place at the right time. This stops being a measure of *our* ability or inability, and shifts towards being a manifestation of *His* ability.

True religion is about reciprocating the love that we have already been shown.

The 'pool-gazing hopeful' in this story leaves the 'House of competition' carrying his rolled-up sleeping mat tucked under his arm. He walks away simply expressing God's interruption into his circumstances.

Unfortunately though, this doesn't seem to last.

ROOTED

Transference. Conversion.

One is just movement, the other is change. One is concerned with location, the other is about substance. One is anxious in seeking, while the other dwells. One measures growth by experiences, the other by fruit. One is an echo of the other's unique expression.

There's a sad ending to this unnamed man's story in John 5. At the end of the passage, Jesus finds this man in the Temple – who knows why he's there? Maybe he's there because he's thankful to God for what has happened in his life that day. This would be great; this would appear to be grace leading to obedience, love leading to love – Conversion.

However, I offer an alternative interpretation – maybe the man has just gone from one mechanical system to another mechanical system. My reason for thinking this? – Why else would he be so eager to snitch on Jesus to the religious leaders of his day?

He's eager to meet the demands of the new system that he has found himself part of. Let's be honest – the minute this man was free, the 'ripple experts' of this other system were on him with demands, rules and regulations. And their methods of persuasion are so effective that the man is taken in by it, suckered into believing that *he's* not meeting what's required.

What we see in this man is Transference.

Within moments of Jesus liberating him, he forgets what he has received and walks willingly into another pool. Instead of living in the revelation of God's love for him, and the freedom this produces, he now finds himself once again trying to earn acceptance, trying to find an approvable way to obtain what he literally tasted for just a few moments prior. It's ironic that it was Jesus who gave this man his legs back, only for him to then use those same legs to run and report Jesus to the authorities.

He's become snared into another lifestyle of wave-waiting.

Maybe this is what Jesus was talking about, when he warns the man at the end of the passage about 'sin' and 'something worse happening to him'[5] – we often read this as if Jesus was threatening him with another infirmity if he steps out of line! But what if Jesus' 'something worse' isn't sickness, but more systematic living?

Paul writes in one of his letters to the early church, early experiencers of this freedom of Jesus –

> *'As you therefore have received Christ*
> *Jesus the Lord, so walk in him...'[6]*

Think about this for just a second – how did we receive Jesus? – By grace. So how do I walk in him (i.e. obey him)?

It's funny that even though I know I am saved by grace, I still end up forgetting this when it comes to the practice of following Jesus. It's almost as if I treat grace like an invitation to audition, when it's more like winning first prize even though I didn't perform.

Personally, I'm not much different from this man we read about in John 5. I can easily overlook the grace I have been shown and begin reconstructing my old superstitious practices: believing my righteousness counts, thinking that my good works are what maintains the difference. In a nutshell, I take my freedom and run back to law. I leave the pool and I enter the temple – leaving Jesus somewhere in between and putting trust back into my own observance. My problem is that I am used to something being demanded of me; I forget that I am in need of what Jesus provides at every stage in this journey and not what I feel I contribute to it (which isn't anything anyway). Maybe I'm not alone in this forgetfulness? Thankfully, like in the story, Jesus always finds us, reminding us of what actually brought the change in the first place – His love.

For those who might be panicking right now, this doesn't mean that our works don't have any place, but we need to remember that works are a product, not a precursor; their place is secondary. The difference between our attempts and Jesus' achievement is like the difference between decorating a tree and the beauty of a real tree laden down with fruit in autumn. Actually, trees are a helpful analogy, one that both the Apostle Paul and Jesus used.

For example, after Paul delivers the advice noted above, he continues by encouraging these, and other early believers to allow their *roots* to go down into Jesus and draw nourishment from him (Colossians 2:7), and to come to an understanding '…as all God's people should, [of] how wide, how long, how high and how deep [Jesus'] love really is' (Ephesians 3:18, NLT). Paul encourages us to *plant* ourselves in Jesus, to go deep into the soil of God's love and explore its dimensions.

I'm not a gardener, I don't possess the gift of 'green fingers', but I do know a few small things about the biology and anatomy of plants – one thing that instantly stands out is that roots are not legs. This may surprise you, but I've never seen the tree in our garden at home pull itself up, and move to a sunnier patch. It's rooted – it's not interested in the experiences travel brings, it's only interested in the depth of the earth beneath it. Plants 'know' that within the ground beneath them, the same ground that nurtured and gave birth to them, lies all the nourishment they require to develop. Everything a tree is and produces is a manifestation, a *conversion*, of the ground that it roots itself into.

Jesus uses similar imagery, except that we're not described as *the* tree, but an extension of it, an extension of Jesus: 'Remain in me, and I will remain in you. For a branch cannot produce anything if it is severed from the vine, and you cannot be fruitful apart from me'[7]. This is a deeper imagery than just knowing about Jesus and learning about Jesus. This remaining is relational, forming a permanent connection to Him, allowing what He is to be passed into us, His nature coursing through our nature.

This is no longer some mechanical system – where we wait for movement, only to respond with a movement. This is an organic system – where what we do, and what we are, is an extension of the substance we are planted in.

Maybe I am thinking about this too simplistically, after all I am a simple person. But from my perspective, obedience to Jesus is all about being *rooted* in Jesus; It's not so much about copying him, but about expressing him.

Brennan Manning phrases it like this –

> *'Imitation could be a question of isolated actions; identification with Jesus touches the root of our actions, the principles by which we habitually judge and decide'*[8]

MORE LOVE

I'm not perfect. Seriously, I mess up big time. There are things I have done that do not reflect the nature that Jesus possesses. I'm still going through this process of learning to trust, to place and keep my roots into Jesus. But I've come to realise a pattern in my life – I am more prone to mess up, to forget my new nature, when I forget how much I am loved by Him.

Transfer season in my life often occurs when life goes wrong, when problems creep in, and storms cover every conceivable horizon. I don't have any issues with believing in God's existence (at least, not anymore), but there have been numerous times when I have doubted His goodness. It's in those moments when I'm always tempted to pull up my roots and 'make like a tree...' (Sorry for the pun).

Ultimately, what results is that I begin to sink back into the movements of the water's currents. Like Peter, the disciple, when he first stepped out of the boat, too many years in the system have given me this horrible habit of placing false confidence in my own ability to respond to the motion of the waves instead of trusting Jesus' ability to transcend them. My life once again starts to respond to the ebb and flow of my circumstances instead of the steadfast love of God.

I can't be harsh with the man we read about in John chapter 5 – incidentally, Jesus isn't either – I can totally understand the healed man's choice to be a part of a system once again. A system is understandable. There's an addiction we all have to things that appear to make systematic sense, whereas, God's unconditional love doesn't – especially when a crisis hits.

When the tough times roll, our mechanical thinking can begin to take over; we feel that something must be off with our input to have caused all the pain and trauma that surrounds us. So we react, compensating with more spiritual 'spin' and 'saliva', hoping that our efforts can calm the storm. There's another story there that we could take a look at if we had the time; suffice it to say that when we react in this way, we're right on par with the disciples in their storm-beset boat – we're moved by fear, not love. We fear God has overlooked us, that He's ceased loving us, that He's abandoned us. Maybe sometimes we reinforce this by thinking that He's justified in doing so.

When I review myself, I always fail to understand how God can love me. I know *me*, and I know that God sees the 'me' that others are blind to. The maths just don't add up, I can't figure it out, and so I find it difficult to anchor myself to something, or someone, whose reactions are totally independent of my actions. I find it equally difficult to believe that they would choose to anchor themselves to me. But He does love us, He is committed to us (and to the whole of creation) – His life, His death on a cross, and His resurrection boldly declares His passionate faithfulness to all life.

When we observe the cross, we realise that we are totally helpless to save ourselves. But Jesus doesn't call us, like the waters, to offer what we do not possess; instead He Himself meets the requirements.

Here's a thought, one that I'm certain you've heard at some point or another – Our actions don't change the way God feels about us. In other words, your actions can never stimulate God to love you more, or disgust God in such a way that he would love you less.

However, maybe our actions do betray how *we feel* God feels about us? Keeping to tree analogies once more, maybe the reason we lack fruit, to grow in obedience, is because we lack roots?

I apologise in advance for what I am just about to say, but a scene from the movie *'The Empire Strikes Back'* comes to mind (That's a *Star Wars* film by the way, the fifth episode – the second film, not the fifth film for the unenlightened out there). The scene is where the lovable rogue Han Solo (played by Harrison Ford) is about to be frozen alive in Carbonite, so he can be delivered as a trophy to the notorious Tattooine gangster Jabba the Hutt. The process is like having a spray tan, but with a more serious and paler looking effect. Just as Han (to his friends) is about to be lowered into the freezer, and over the noise of the machines and Chewbacca's infamous growling-chuckling-gargling cry, Carrie Fisher's Princess Leia shouts, *'I love you'*. To which a very calm and collected Solo replies, *'I know'* (which is his roguish way of saying 'I love you too').

Do we really understand that God loves us? I mean, that He is more than fond of us, He is passionately committed to us? Do we understand that, as Paul writes in his letter *Romans*, that 'nothing can separate us from God's love'? If you do, then maybe like me, you have this desire to live in such a way that when Jesus shouts 'I love you' over the storms in life, our lives shout back 'I know'.

I'm convinced that the solution to our obedience 'problems' is not more rules, regulations or rituals, but more love. Or to be more specific, more acknowledgement of the love we have received. Love is the fertilizer we require to impregnate us with the willingness and power to obey. Obedience grows, where love is reciprocated.

IF YOU LOVE ME...

'If you loved me, then you would/wouldn't...' Just hearing the words makes us cringe. When someone uses love in such a context then it's almost natural to suspect that they are using it as an attempt to camouflage getting their own way. Something in us automatically raises

our guard, our minds switch to defence mode, even our posture and facial expression change – we're receptive, but extremely cautious.

So I can't really blame my five year old son for pulling his face the way he did when I was 'asking' him to 'do what Daddy says'. I'm not the best Dad in the world, or even in my locality. So I'll be honest with you, I do use love in this context from time to time in my pep talks to my kids – either, in an attempt to get them to tidy their rooms, or to let me have a turn on the computer game, or to teach them about why they shouldn't just say 'I love you' and then the next minute turn into grumpy immovable monsters in the middle of a supermarket (really, how do children increase their body weight in such an exponential way?) So, there are times when I say 'If you loved me...' to get my way, but there are times when I am honestly trying to teach my children an important truth about relationships; Love is demonstrated through devotion.

I'm not talking about blind devotion that discourages us to think for ourselves, nor am I talking about the kind of romantic sloppy love that causes people not to think things through properly. Neither am I talking about the kind of love that is so distorted that it fails to see the true intentions of the one that it is devoted to. And to be clear, I am not talking about the kind of devotion that is demanded, and produces an environment where abuse is carried out.

I don't believe *true* devotion can be demanded – it can only be given, and only as an act of love in response to being loved.

Obedience may not be a popular word these days – and I can understand why, especially given the word's history of use as justification of atrocities such as abuse and violence within marriage. However, despite the misapplication of this word by others, it is a word that Jesus uses and so we must wrestle with what this means.

Within John 14, part of the gospel's description of the events taking place at the last supper, Jesus clearly connects obedience to an act of love;

'If you love me, obey my commandments' – John 14:15 (NLT)

'Those who obey my commandments are the ones who love me' – John 14:21 (NLT)

'All those who love me will do what I say' – John 14:23 (NLT)

'Anyone who doesn't love me will not do what I say' – John 14:24 (NLT)

So there it is; the infamous 'if you love me...' line. It seems pretty clear to Jesus, that an expression of love is obedience. But before we think that Jesus is trying to manipulate us with getting His way, we really need to see the situation He is in when He delivers these words.

Jesus has just finished washing the disciple's twenty-four dirty feet – twenty-four feet at least. Two dozen, rotten, smelly soles that had spent the whole day walking around the dusty, unclean streets of Judea.

The basin of dirty, used water is probably lying on the floor close by, with the floor of the meeting room still showing the signs of where adult feet have splashed out some of its contents. A damp towel, that girded Jesus' waist a few minutes earlier, still lies close to His hands, and the clothing under His robes is still damp and stained with the filth that once covered His friends' feet.

This is a Holy moment. But not the kind that we conjure in our heads – a time full of incense, candles and chanting harmonies – a moment so pure that we get goosebumps. This is Holy, and maybe in a way that offends us – it's dirty, sweaty and smelly.

This is such a ridiculous picture, if we'll take a moment to consider it. Washing feet was a servant's job, the lowest person's role. Washing feet is where you started and where you hoped to be promoted from, this is not where careers end – but this is what Jesus had decided to do. And, it's not that Jesus has had a moment of identity crisis – John tells us that prior to picking up the towel 'Jesus knew that the Father had given Him authority over everything...'[9], and as a result of such knowledge, Jesus chooses to exercise His authority by serving – not dictating. This is what Jesus does with power and status! He doesn't seek to seize control. He doesn't flex His equality with God in order to dominate and demand. Instead, He pours out a bowl of water, girds His waist with a towel, and takes hold of the feet of His friends in His own hands. As an act of love, He gives them an example and not an ultimatum. Paul would later remind the church of this example:

> 'Though he was God, he did not demand and cling to
> his rights as God. He made himself nothing...'[10]

No wonder Simon Peter refuses and tells Jesus that there's not a chance that he's going to allow Him to wash his feet! This was scandalous – the Teacher washing feet, the miracle worker washing camel muck from between people's toes, the Messiah giving manicures.

We may chuckle at Peter's protest, but I often wonder – if Jesus began to wash my feet, would I protest like Peter, or would I think that this is where Jesus should be? Is Jesus the One with the authority, or is His primary role about servicing my requirements and cleaning up my mess?

Again, it's a question of control, but once more Jesus isn't coaxed into this, or manipulated into this – the whole scene is an act of His love for His friends, even for one who would betray him.

So when Jesus says, 'if you love me...' within this context, this isn't a statement from a man trying to manipulate people, and who is trying to stamp His authority. He's simply stating a truth about relationships – that love expresses itself through obedience. He's not saying that we need to obey Him to be loved by Him – He has already shown His commitment and love to these disciples, and will go on to give yet another, even greater display of that love. What Jesus is saying is that we should never expect ourselves to obey anything He asks of us if we don't love Him. And, as discussed earlier, that love for Him will only ever flow out of an acknowledgement that He, first of all, loves us.

It's interesting that God doesn't demonstrate to us why we should obey him through a display of His destructive power. Alternatively, He 'stamps' His authority as He surrenders His life on a cross, and He demonstrates His glory through His re-creative act of resurrection. True power, is not displayed through the ability to destroy, but through the ability to create. J.Robert Oppenheimer ("Father of the Atomic Bomb") famously said: 'I have become death, the destroyer of worlds', but Jesus declared: 'I am the resurrection and the life'[11].

It's this use of power that gets my attention, this display of power that gets my allegiance, especially when the One who wields such authority, would love me enough that He would be willing to come and bend down to clean the dirt from underneath my toe nails. To such love, I surrender.

FINAL THOUGHT

Maybe I haven't said enough. Maybe you're wondering why I have spent so much time talking about the motive and source of obedience rather than the actual practice/act of obedience. If it helps you, then some of that will permeate the discussions in other chapters of this book such as WORSHIP, SERVICE and LEARNING etc... although I might not explicitly mention the word obedience.

I felt it important that we spent this time touching the heart, as it's from there that our expression flows. There is something I need you to understand at the very start of this book – that this book is not about salvation, this book is not about getting a response out of God, or trying to earn His love/approval. It is about responding to His love, living to honour Him through expressing the love that he has already shown to us.

You cannot work for God.

You cannot bribe Him with your commitment.

You cannot 'woo' the creator with your dedication or ability to watch ripples.

Your attendance doesn't impress Him.

You can't *do* anything...

...except surrender.

Surrender to a Love that is greater than our infirmities, and imperfections, and immorality.

Surrender to a Love that is more effective than our self-righteousness, our bling, and our saliva-coated spirituality.

We need to remember that it isn't Jesus who teaches that, 'Good things come to those who wait' – remembering once again the taunt of the waters' allure. Using the example of a tree producing good fruit, Jesus teaches us that, 'Good deeds come from a good heart...'[12]. And, fulfilling the words of the prophets, it's a new heart that Jesus has come to give us[13].

However, I can understand it if you want something practical to do after closing this chapter. If that is the case, then the following observation made by Earl Jabay about the rich young ruler who visited Jesus (Matt 19:16, Mark 10:17, Luke 18:18) may be something worth considering:

> *'This man kept the commandments perfectly, but when our Lord suggested new terms, namely, that he sell all his possessions and follow Christ, the young man turned away in sorrow. He was prepared only to work hard for God, not to surrender and become obedient, for that would mean an end to living on his own terms'*[14].

So how about it, let's relinquish our control theology, let's abandon the mechanical understandings of a relationship with our Creator, and let's just embrace Him in loving surrender. Instead of closing this chapter with a mind buzzing with tasks and to-do lists, why not take this opportunity to spend some time talking with God, exploring the compost of His love for you, and turning your ears away from the splashing sounds of water and onto the sound of a voice that asks, *'Would you like to get well?'.*

> *'Let anyone who is thirsty come to me and drink. For the scriptures declare that rivers of living water will flow from the heart of those who believe in me'* – John 7:37-38 (NLT)

> *'So now that you know God (or should I say, now that God knows you), why do you want to go back again and become slaves once more to the weak and useless spiritual principles of this world? You are trying to earn favor with God by observing certain days or months or seasons or years. I fear for you. Perhaps all my hard work with you was for nothing...*

> *For when we place our faith in Christ Jesus, there is no benefit in being circumcised or being uncircumcised. What is important is faith expressing itself in love.'* – Galatians 4:9-11, 5:6 (NLT)

EXPRESSED THROUGH **LEARNING**

'What we observe is not nature itself, but nature
exposed to our method of questioning'
Werner Heisenberg[1]

?

Ok, I admit it's an unusual quotation to begin a chapter with, especially within the context of a book about following Jesus and expressing love, but it's one of my favourites.

In its original setting, the quote is about Heisenberg's 'Uncertainty Principle' – a principle which discusses what we can know about the movements of sub-atomic particles, like electrons and quarks. For example, the principle states that the more certain you are of a particle's location the less certain you can be of its velocity – you can either know one with certainty or the other, but not both[2].

That said, I rarely think about the movements of electrons and quarks – at least on a microscopic scale anyway. For me this quote speaks of something simpler and more fundamental – that to make sense of anything at all, whether that's life, nature, myself, or God etc... requires us to ask questions.

We're hard-wired for exploration and thrust into a universe that leaves us no other choice but to interact with it. Every second of every day, from the moment of our birth (and prior to this), our senses are stimulated with shapes, colours, textures, tastes, aromas and sounds – all of which our brains capture, sort and process – leaving us to then form opinions and conclusions, which carry the potential to become choices and responses (or remain as just plain trivia). But even though we're predisposed to engage with this world, we're not predetermined with how we will interpret it – and sadly, we don't always agree.

We're all subjective people. We could all watch the same film (say *Spider-Man 3*) and all walk away with very different opinions[3]. We all have different ideas about what makes *good* music, or *great* food, or *amazing* experiences. We sample life like a panel of judges and food critics on a cookery show – how we choose to load our fork, what side of the mouth we use to chew our food with, and how much water we use to rinse our palate, all impacts the experience we get. 'There is no end of the opinions ready to be expressed'[4] because we all expose reality to our own methods of questioning.

This isn't to imply that there isn't anything objective, but in order to really experience reality we need to expose it to more than just our own interrogation.

How we have chosen to engage with reality and which/whose questions we have exposed reality to, have played a major part in shaping the people we have become. *Who? What? When? Where? Why?* and *How?* still continue to be powerful tools in sculpting the identities of individuals and societies. Through just this basic set of questions individuals have made extraordinary discoveries and advancements, exposed prejudices and injustice, created opportunities and brought about freedom. On the flip side, by limiting these questions, by placing boundaries on what can be questioned, others have imposed oppression, disguised truth, and distorted growth.

A question carries the potential to be powerful and life-changing, but if used incorrectly, it also carries the possibility of being impotent.

Questions exist for the sole purpose of calling us to investigate, discover and grow. So I find it heart-breaking when I meet people who have allowed questions to cause them to stagnate, people who do nothing with a question, except repeat it to themselves, and others, as an excuse for their complacency. Instead of the question calling them on to something further, something deeper, it becomes a reason to stop searching altogether. It's almost as if they feel that having any sort of question is an indication that they are treading down the wrong path – surely, they believe, the road to truth is filled with answers.

Apart from those car journeys when my sons like to play the 'why' game, I have no issues with people who have questions – it's our natural state. It's not that I'm naively longing for the day when these people finally have the answers, I just want to meet them when they have a more developed question – but their question never grows; they refuse to let themselves be led by the question into the journey of enquiry.

Why does having questions upset us so much?

Asking questions is not a crime, it's not a sinful thing to do, and encountering a question is not a sign of misdirection – we should never see it as a bad thing to hold a question, grow familiar with it and allow it to motivate us. However, not doing anything with a question should be illegal. And it's worth saying to the religious among us, that faith is not the absence of questions; faith is the assurance that our questions have answers, and is the description of the movement from one to the other.

=

Maybe this discomfort with questions has developed because we have the wrong expectations of answers.

It often seems that I live in a culture that expects every answer to fit within a 'sound-bite', or a fifty word synopsis. Answers that fail to be squeezed into *Twitter's* limit of one-hundred and forty characters are treated as suspect, even though we're all aware that life's deepest realities require more explanation than a simple 'yes' or 'no'.

Consider this. My bio on *Twitter* reads as follows: *'Husband to Steph, Father to Corban and Eaden, Follower of Christ, Pastor @mccbury, Friend to Some, Unknown by Many, and Lover of Cadburys!'*[5], but outside of a few facts, this doesn't tell you anything about me at all. We're all so much more complicated than any social site's bio or status gives us room to say. It could potentially take a lifetime of discovery for you and I to really *know* each other – and even then, we would still have questions.

And, that's just you and I – two people in a growing global population comprising approximately seven billion people – who all live on a spinning rock we call earth – a place full of differing chemical combinations forming everything from 'dust-bunnies' and blue whales to the human brain. The earth, a planet which measures 12,756 km in diameter, travelling at a velocity of 108,000 km/h on an elliptical orbit of 365.242 days around a star, a star which is approximately 147-152 million km away from us. This star, our sun, which sits just off the centre of our solar system, is only one of the potential 100 – 400 billion stars that exist within the galaxy called the Milky-Way, which is just one galaxy out of the billions that exist within a universe that some approximate to be ninety-two billion light years in size. A universe that we are beginning to discover is made up of five percent 'light' matter, twenty-five percent dark matter and seventy percent dark energy – and all of this is made up of the movements and interactions of smaller, sub-atomic constituents like electrons, photons and quarks, which are all buzzing around in probabilistic movements that prevent us from being able to fully comprehend their locations and velocities at the same time.

Try and place how all of that works within a sound-bite!

I get it. It's tempting to long for answers that are easy to swallow and that make sense without needing to challenge our thought patterns – and maybe to safeguard and protect ourselves from answers we feel might threaten to do this; then it's also tempting for us to manipulate the results by controlling 'how' we ask the questions.

We place this huge burden on answers to function as finish lines, when they more naturally perform as milestones. We fool ourselves if we believe that answers are the proper response to questions, when the formal acknowledgment of a question is to embrace its invitation to enter into the journey of learning.

TENACITY OR TENANCY

So what? You may be wondering why we're talking about questions, and what any of this has to do with expressing love – so let's pull back just a little bit.

An important facet of love is that it's *other*-interested (it can be *me*-interested too, and not in a self-indulgent way – but let's keep on *other*).

To love is to be fascinated, to wonder, to be intellectually stimulated; love longs to *know* and so moves us beyond the starting blocks of a question and compels us into the course of discovery. Let's face it; apathy is not a description of love.

To learn is to express love.

So when Jesus is asked about the greatest commandment, and he responds with a quote from Deuteronomy 6:5, it shouldn't come as a surprise to find that an aspect of loving God is to love him with our minds[6].

Maybe, for some of us, we think Jesus is talking about keeping our brains clear of impure thoughts. We imagine that our head is like a room that God wants to rent, so we work hard to keep it in a fit, liveable state, dust free and hypoallergenic for our assumedly sin-sensitive-allergic-deity-tenant. But then 'Doh!' – we briefly noticed that *Wonderbra* billboard advertisement on the way to work, and 'Doh!' a work colleague said something inappropriate which now finds itself stuck on repeat in our head, and 'Doh!' another driver cut us up on the journey home and revenge scenarios play over in our minds etc...

I don't know about you, but I fail at this kind of thing every day. I live in a world that never ceases to bombard my senses and I continue to struggle with the ability to filter everything that comes my way and, as shocking as this may sound to some people, my brain hasn't developed the ability to place automatic censor strips on images and nice timely 'beeps' into other people's conversations. But seriously, do we really expect not to 'see' or 'hear'? Do we really expect to live in sensory disconnect from the world in which we live, the multi-sensory world that God created, purposed and loves? Would this actually be a godly response to the world around us? Did Jesus live this way? And what if it's not so much to do with *what* we're thinking about, but *how* we are thinking about it?

The heart is right; I do want to honour God with my thinking. Like the psalmist I long for my thoughts to be pleasing to Him (Psalm 19:14), but my methodology is faulty – I will always fail at trying to play landlord to God, especially as that keeps me in charge.

But what if loving God with our brains was much simpler and much more effective than self-sterilisation? What if loving God with our minds was more about allowing ourselves to be mentally stimulated by Him, and allowing Him to shape how we think? After all, it's possible to be good at housekeeping, but awful at hospitality. Let's put it this way:

> Do we think about God?
> Are we fascinated with Him?
> Does the mystery of who He is call us to explore who He is?
> Do we wonder at His ways?
> Do we feel He has anything to teach us?
> Do our prayers contain questions about Him, or just statements that have been learnt by rote?

This might sound like a counter-intuitive thing to say, but could having questions about God (questions that are actually pursued) be more of an expression of love than thinking we have all the answers? Could a mind stimulated, and in pursuit of God be more 'pleasing' to him than a mind that is swept clean and vacant?

And, considering what Jesus says further about the 'second and equally important' commandment, when quoting Leviticus 19:18, shouldn't loving our neighbour also mean wanting to *know* them as well? And what methodologies do we adopt in going about this discovery? Listening to gossip and rumours, running background checks, searching social sites, rummaging through their rubbish and digging up their past? Or should our longing to *know* actually move us into real, direct, and present relationship?

I've talked about questions, answers, and intellect, but please understand that this chapter isn't about growing bigger brains; the goal here is deeper relationships. Although it's important to gain knowledge, the focus of expressing love through learning is not about collecting data and figures and facts. Even though this desire for knowledge may begin within our minds, it will also grow to include our heart, strength and soul. Knowing God, and others, can't be done by just gleaning information from study books or searching websites while remaining distant – this learning can only happen while experiencing something of their presence.

Relationships are the only means open to us to really discover each other in a truly human and divine way. Love expressed through learning will always move us into communion.

> *'Love, when it is the love of which the Johannine Jesus speaks so frequently is the mode of knowing in which the object of love is fully affirmed, cherished and valued, but in which simultaneously the knower is fully involved as a delighted, appreciative, celebratory participant.'*[7]

I have to be honest and ask myself something at this point; I can potentially spend hours flitting through twitter profiles in an attempt to discover people and their insights; I can be prone to reading the occasional quantum mechanics book in an attempt to understand how this world works; but when was the last time I looked at Jesus and found myself repeating the disciples' question, 'Who is this man?'[8] and where did I allow this question to lead me?

LORD OF THE WATERS

Try and picture the scene. Jesus is teaching about the Kingdom of God from a boat – maybe he's talking about the *Be-attitudes*, or telling stories like that of the *Lost Coins* or the *Pearl Merchant*, or taking questions from the crowd and responding with answers, or more stories, or with questions of his own. It's one huge learning fest; the crowds communing with Jesus, Jesus communing with the crowds[9].

During all of this Peter sits at the back of his boat, keeping it steady in its location on the water, while watching and listening as the teacher talks about the scriptures and the heart of God. Despite having his boat requisitioned by Jesus, Peter must have been impressed with what he was seeing and hearing. After all, it takes skill to hold an audience the size Jesus had. Seriously, Jesus must have been pretty good at this!

Maybe Peter, as he's viewing all this, would begin to remember the events that took place when Jesus was once a guest at his home; when Jesus healed Peter's mother-in-law who was suffering from a serious fever (see Luke 4:38-41). You can imagine the glint of wonder in Peter's eyes as he thinks back to that night; as he remembers all the other sick people in his village coming to be healed too. And here He is again, this 'man of God'; sat in *his* boat, using it as a platform to teach the crowds that have gathered. He was *very* good at this – when it came to 'God', this Jesus knew His stuff; He had authority. He would have had Peter's respect too.

The teaching eventually comes to an end, the crowds begin to depart – maybe a few people linger hoping for an encore – and then Jesus turns to Peter and asks him to go on a fishing trip.

Sorry, did I say 'asks'? When you read the text this isn't much of a question – maybe the better way to term it would be 'commands'. Jesus, the teacher, turns to Simon, the fisherman and, using non-descriptive terms *commands* him to go out and get the catch of his life.

Now, seriously and honestly, if you were Peter, what would you think?

I ask this because I think there are a lot of ideas out there that Peter's response to this prompt is a statement of faith – maybe I'm wrong (and I'm happy to be so), but I don't see it that way. If it helps you, let's take a detour for a moment...

Pretend you're a heart surgeon – not just any heart surgeon, but the best in the world. You're famous, acclaimed – so much so, that you are constantly being harassed to share your insights and expertise at international conferences and within the pages of medical journals. You even have your own branch of medical centres, which specialise in the latest and most cutting edge treatments of the day. You're at the top of your game, the top in your field.

That said, we're realists here, so we sadly admit that not every surgery is successful – sometimes, despite the greatest of efforts, the best skill, and the most up to date technological advancements, some people just don't make it.

Today is one of those days for you. You've just come out of a five hour surgery, you've given the best of everything you've got – but this patient isn't going to come through. You could carry on surgery for a few more hours but you, more than anyone else in the world, know that this is a lost cause. Sadly, some things are out of your control.

Now imagine, that while you're busy scrubbing up, rehearsing over and over in your mind how you will break this tragic news to awaiting loved ones, I suddenly I turn up. And I *tell* you to get back into surgery and you *will* save that patient's life. At first you'd be so stunned, I doubt you would be speedily donning the surgical gloves. You might try to explain to me that it's hopeless, that despite the best tech and latest procedures and the best brains on the task, there is nothing that can be done, but eventually (and I imagine much sooner than later), you would want to know how *I* could be so confident in such a statement – which would ultimately revolve around the question of who I was.

I'm a Structural Engineer, my work deals with the design and construction of steelwork buildings. In my field of expertise we mess about with stresses, inertias, bending moments, 'charpy v-notch' values, bio-metallic corrosion, wind loadings and so forth... in short, I deal with metal, not flesh (by the way, I'm not play acting here, that's actually what I do for a living). I then go on to tell you, the leading expert in heart surgeries, that I have been in the construction sector since leaving school, and I begin to show you a portfolio of my work – all in the hope of demonstrating my proficiency in my field of expertise and earning your respect.

Now, as the world's foremost expert in heart surgery, regardless of me having your respect or not, would you take my statement seriously and get back into the operation theatre?

So, back to the story...

Peter's an expert too! He's a partner in his own business – he's a professional. He has fished in these waters since childhood – he would know the effects that each season of the year would have on the currents and tides of this particular sea – he would know what species of fish live in these waters and where he would be mostly likely to find them at each particular time of day. What you and I would just describe as the Sea of Galilee, Peter would describe as being made up of much smaller areas; all having their own place names, all mapped out and charted in his mind (in other words, it isn't just *shallow* or *deep*).

On top of that, Peter is also tired, he's worn out and disappointed with the extremely bad results of a hard night's work – this is not the best frame of mind to catch anybody in. Prior to Jesus turning up, he was busy with cleaning his nets and packing away before his return trip home.

If you were Peter, how would you respond to this ex-carpenter turned Rabbi's command to go get the catch of your career – especially when he uses a non-descriptive location like 'where it's deeper'? Jesus obviously had Peter's respect, but what could this expert in 'God' teach him about fishing?

Peter's response shouldn't really come as a surprise; after reminding Jesus that He is a respected Teacher (by calling him Master), Peter pulls no punches in bringing his professional opinion to the table –

'We [the experts] worked hard...

... All night...

... And still didn't catch a thing'[10].

Maybe I'm being cynical, but I don't hear Simon Peter's *'But, If you say so...'* as a statement of faith. Maybe I'm wrong, but after reading him defend his expertise as a fisherman, I detect a sense of sarcasm – 'But if *you* say so, after all what do *I* know about fishing!'

But Peter chooses to go. Why? Some might suggest that Peter took a step of faith, knowing that something fantastic was just about to happen. But that just doesn't make sense, because holding such a hope certainly doesn't match with Peter's response. What Peter encounters, he certainly wasn't expecting...

> *'When Simon Peter realized what had happened, he fell to his knees before Jesus and said, "Oh, Lord, please leave me – I'm too much of a sinner to be around you". For he was awestruck by the size of their catch, as were the others with him. His partners, James and John, the sons of Zebedee, were also amazed.*
> *Jesus replied to Simon, "Don't be afraid! From now on you'll be fishing for people!"'*[11]

Isn't it funny that Jesus never got this kind of response when He healed Peter's mother-in-law! Now ok, maybe Peter just didn't get on with his mother-in-law, but I suspect it was something more poignant than that.

Peter thought that he could teach Jesus something.

As far as he was concerned, when it came to the 'God stuff' – healings, teaching scripture – then Jesus was *it*, and Peter was a big fan. But in the day-to-day stuff, like earning a living... Peter knew best. But what Jesus did, made Peter think twice about who was really 'Lord over the waters'.

Peter's spent his life learning the movements of these waters, these currents are how he earns his life – he's worked hard trying to be in the right place, at the right time to get his dreams dispensed. And then Jesus shows up, and produces something that Peter's best efforts could never have achieved (In many ways this story is a lot like the one we looked at in the previous chapter).

Grace breaks in again. Peter's labours are overtaken by divine grace. And concealed within this usurping act is the summons to rethink his opinion of Jesus. Experiencing something of the grace of God should always cause our self-perceived ideas about 'Who He is' and 'How He works' to pop.

Let's not be hard on Peter, haven't we all thought this at some point – that we are more informed in one particular sphere of our lives than Jesus is? Even though we sing songs to Him and about Him every week in church services, even though we love Him because He loves us, even though we call Him 'The Truth' – don't we all, at some level, think we know best?

Have we, with our incorrect separation of 'Spiritual Life' from 'Physical Life', placed Jesus as 'Master' of the eternal only, while we remain 'Master' of the earthly? This is pretty important stuff to ask if we're talking about learning from Jesus. After all, does Jesus have anything to teach us? Who is the expert when the topic is *'my'* life'? If the answer is Jesus, then how does this affect our interrogation of reality, and what do we do with the information He provides?

Dallas Willard, in his book *The Great Omission*, notes a worrying trend amongst those who profess to follow Jesus; '*Many Christians do not even think of him [Jesus] as one with reliable information about their lives. Consequently they do not become his students*'[12]. They relegate Jesus and His teaching to the substitution bench, while they attentively study the wisdom, and invest in the life-style choices of those who have already succeeded down the roads that they wish to travel.

This is scary if true. But Pastor Willard wouldn't be the first person in history to note this disconnection between Jesus and those who claim to worship Him; it's a disconnection that is birthed from our answer to 'Who is this man?'

If Jesus is nothing more to us than a teacher of morals, then he's one of a thousand 'life coaches' and perspectives to choose from – most are happy to take a few of his statements and put them on motivational posters, alongside Gandhi, Winston Churchill and Homer (Simpson, that is). If he's *just* a spokesman for the marginalised then it's great, on the one hand, that we are called to review how we view and treat the rest of humanity, but what about when he talks about our relationship with God? If Jesus is just some kind of cynic, then he becomes just another voice to glean quotes from for our own critiques of sociological and political evils.

But, what if He is 'Lord'? What if He is actually 'God in Flesh'? What if He has an agenda, and His own kingdom? Then our call is not just to hear and applaud, but to understand and to respond.

Peter's experience of grace opens his eyes to see Jesus as one who isn't his equal, but as someone who is his superior. What Peter realises while waist deep in a pile of flapping stinking fish, causes him to stop calling Jesus 'Master' and moves him to address Jesus as 'Lord'. Peter stops trying to be the teacher, and becomes a student.

DISCO

The word *disciple* is not as scary as it sounds. Sadly, it's a word that is often tied in with being 'fanatical' or 'radicalised', but our world is full of wannabes – everyone wants to be like somebody else. And if that thought offends you, or maybe you feel that definition doesn't fit (and maybe it doesn't), then a further truth is that there are plenty of people that you don't want to be like.

And it doesn't just stop with people; even things inspire characteristics in us. We don't just have *likes*, we have *loves*. From football, to soap operas, to social sites, to computer games, to work, to food, to education – we all have those things that we invest ourselves into. On many levels 'we are what we eat' – this is the stuff that we not only ingest, but digest; it's these things that fuel us, form us, and define our movements.

I remember walking to school with one of my brothers. I had just started secondary school and he was in his final year. Being much older gave him a considerable height advantage which he still naturally maintains. Have you ever tried walking alongside someone who has a clear two feet height advantage over you? His one small step was my giant leap. He would take his strides, whereas I would take a step, followed by a small jog, a step, another jog... by the time I got to school I would be soaked in sweat. However, the more time you spend walking with someone, the more you learn to walk like they do – I learnt to keep pace, which led to the not-so-positive side-effect of resetting my natural walking default to fast.

As time moves on, who you walk with inevitably changes. My wife is shorter than me – she won't appreciate me telling you that, especially as I'm not a tall person – so when we were dating I found myself having to slow down to save her from the jogging and to save myself from the ear-ache. As strange as it sounds, it wasn't an easy task to gear down, I had to really think about it – imagine that, I had to think about how to walk! Now I'm a Dad, I have two boys whose walking speeds vary erratically depending upon our destination – sweet-shop or school could be more easily described as fifth gear or reverse – so yet again, my mind has to engage with my walk.

In all these instances, it's the nature of my relationship with these people that causes me to re-evaluate my movements in relation to theirs.

You only have to observe a crowd on a busy shopping day – you can tell who's with who, and how they feel about the person they are with, all through just watching their walks. Picture the small child lagging six steps behind his dad, with his hands thrust in his pockets and a grumpy look on his face. It doesn't take an Einstein to tell you that he thinks his daddy is being unfair because he won't buy him that *Skylanders* figure (It's a common scene in this current season of my life). Our walks talk.

When love is expressed through learning, it will always be reflected in our movement.

We shouldn't be mistaken then when it comes to learning from Jesus. He doesn't just call us to be his friends, or his fans, or even his followers in a social networking sense. Jesus' claim to be 'The Way, The Truth and The Life' moves him beyond a batch of data and facts, or an idea to analyse, to *the* person to engage with and *the* relationship to be formed by. The experience of his grace challenges the movements of our life,

> *'True religion is not our desperate search to make God intelligible. It is a response to what God has spoken. And the words of God are far more than divine information – they are life to the listener.'*[13]

The Latin root of the word *disciple* – which means 'to study' – is the word *'disco'*[14]. I love this imagery; that to learn is to move in rhythm with something, to observe and to repeat, to respond to its motion.

Jesus came to teach us how to truly live, not just in some spiritual sense, but in the real physical stuff. He came to not only show us what God is like, but also what being human means. He came to demonstrate to us what it is to be made in the likeness of the divine – an image that was never intended to be a clay version of a selfie that God took in years past, but a continual reflection of his eternal movements. Jesus came to teach us how to dance in a world that has lost its tempo. He calls us to repeat his rhythm, to express his movements and to teach others the way via our imitation of him.

Jesus didn't live, die and resurrect just to receive our applause, but to win our allegiance.

This call to express love through learning is not just a challenge to learn *about* Jesus, but *from* Jesus. He wants to reset our default. It seems that to express love through learning is also, paradoxically, a call to express love through unlearning.

But how long will this take?

'I KNOW KUNG FU...'

In some ways, it would be great to live in the technological world shown to us in the film *The Matrix*. All that is required to learn something new is a computer, the capacity to plug a cable into the back of your head and the push of a button – through this process alone, *Neo* (played by Keanu Reeves) learns the martial art of Kung Fu. He doesn't have to attend any rigorous training sessions year after year. He doesn't require the help of any mentors or sparring partners. *Neo* never has to experience the sting of failure, or feel the agony of overworked muscles – he doesn't even have to break into a sweat. It sounds great. Just think of what we could know if all it took was a download.

I doubt I'm alone in this, but there are a great number of things I would love to know and be able to do.

For example, my father-in-law used to be a car body builder. I don't mean someone who physically works out by lifting *Volkswagens* (other car manufacturers are available), but someone who repairs the shells of damaged motor vehicles. Because of this training he's got a pretty good knowledge of how cars work and what needs fixing when they don't. I, on the other hand, know absolutely nothing about cars, something which I am certain disappoints Steph's dad. I know more about football than motor vehicles, which for those who know me will just go to demonstrate how little I know about cars. In the world of the download I could instantly have the ability to change some brake discs, or be able to replace a handbrake cable, or even fix a blown head gasket (I have no idea what that last one is). As well as this earning me a shred of credibility with my father-in-law, such skill would also prevent me getting ripped off by some professional mechanic!

But why stop there?

When I was younger, my tennis racket spent more time being an imaginary guitar than an item of sports equipment. With my music playing on the stereo with the volume and equalizers turned up, my room would transform into a stadium full of invisible, but adoring fans – all shouting and cheering at my technique as I masqueraded as someone like Slash on 'Sweet Child of O' Mine' or Richie Sambora playing 'While my guitar lies bleeding'. To play the actual thing like I did the imaginary one would be a dream come true. But I'm painfully aware that it's already taken me huge quantities of time to develop the movements and calloused fingertips I already possess, producing abilities which barely enable me to play the small handful of guitar chords that I know. I'm so aware of this, that mastering a song like 'November Rain' would, to some extent, feel like a life sentence.

There are things I *want to know* – I want to be able to fix car brakes; I want to be an accomplished musician; I would love to speak fluently in a foreign language (or two) instead of just putting on silly, stereotypical accents; it would be cool to be able to snowboard, or surfboard, or even skateboard... the thing is, *I don't want to learn.*

I want to know, but I don't want to think.

I want to know, but I don't want to practise.

I want to know, but I don't want to listen.

I want to know, but I don't want to sacrifice, sweat, or even risk stumbling.

Sadly, learning is much more of a longer digestive process than a download. As the writer of Proverbs tells us: 'To learn, you must love discipline...' (Proverbs 12:1, NLT).

The Greek root of the word *disciple* is 'math' – which means learning accompanied by endeavour – thinking followed by walking, listening followed by doing, hearing followed by responding. There is no short-cutting our need to participate in this process.

Why does learning have to be so difficult? Because it's the actual process of learning that shapes our character (who we are), whereas a transaction of information just forms intellect (what we know). To paraphrase something the Apostle Paul said: 'Knowledge alone just forms an empty shell, decorative but fragile. But love works to strengthen and develop not only ourselves, but those around us' (see 1 Corinthians 8:1). It's always easier and less messy to hang posters than it is to dig the foundations.

In love we are called to follow Jesus – but that doesn't mean that this is going to be easy, or that we are expected to be perfect overnight. There's room in this to fail. Even though Paul writes that we '...have the mind of Christ', this is not some *Matrix*-style download. Elsewhere Paul has to remind us that 'God is *working* in you, giving you the desire to obey him and the power to do what pleases him'[15]. This journey requires time, all natural growth does. As Sherlock Holme's brother Mycroft (played by Rhys Ifans, in the CBS show *Elementary*) remarks, '...as far as I can see, change is sloppy; it's process not an absolute state'.

Trust is a perfect description of the movement of love expressed through learning. The Old Testament Prophet Isaiah takes the time to tell us that those who trust in God, will find new strength; they will fly... they will run... they will walk[16]. These words remind us that this learning process isn't a race. Learning the walk of Jesus isn't about speed or distance or pace. There will be moments when we will feel like we're soaring, but there will also be moments when we'll trudge – but there's still motion when we tap into His grace, when we trust in His ability usurping our inability; it's there that we find the strength to keep momentum.

I've been in this process fifteen years, and I've had those moments when I feel nothing can get in my way, but I've also had plenty of occasions when I've messed up – big time! This change is sloppy – and that's ok. God's got me in the process. So I'm happy to keep giving myself to this fumbling/stumbling journey of discipleship. Grace calls me onward.

FRUCTUS DIVINAE GRATIAE

The same Peter who professed to Jesus being Lord while knee deep in fish, later encouraged other followers of Jesus to not only *grow* in the *grace* of Jesus, but also in the *knowledge* of Him[17]. It's insightful that Peter encourages people to grow in both; he's aware that without grace, this call to follow, this call to learn will just dissolve into another performance competition – when we 'feel' we are doing well, we'll feel accepted, and when we stumble we'll feel unworthy and drop out – we cannot afford to forget that God has already accepted us.

To echo back to the previous chapter, our expression can only grow from the security of knowing that we are rooted in Jesus – *Grace* and *Growth* must go together. It's only by grace that I have been invited to follow, so my failures in this process won't disqualify me.

This is the beauty of God's grace; it meets us and accepts us right where we are, making no demands on us. And yet, when we experience this illogical grace, it leaves a taste, a strong compulsion to seek out its source. The grace shown to us through Jesus asks us for nothing, but conversely leaves us asking for more. Therefore grace, the unconditional love and undeserved favour of God, becomes our motivation to keep growing and to continue putting down roots, not our excuse to quit.

But, even though grace has no strings attached, Peter goes on to say that there are results when we learn in this way of grace. Another follower of Jesus, James, also reminds us of this:

> 'And remember, it is a message to obey not just to listen to. If you don't obey, you are only fooling yourself... it is like looking at your face in a mirror but doing nothing to improve your appearance. You see yourself, walk away, and forget what you look like.'[18]

James tells us that this learning should cause us to see our image, our expression, and correct it. It's important to note that this call to evaluate our image is deeper than the quality of our cosmetic – it's a reshaping of our hearts.

Why is it, that when we think of examples of obedient people the first thing we mention is their exploits or gifts, but not their fruit? We can focus on their appearance and not their heart. Even with the biblical heroes, Moses, Abram/Abraham, Joseph, David etc. we look at the acts of faith that they performed and fail to notice the character that was being formed within them.

As a Pentecostal, I've met a lot of people who can speak in tongues, but sadly some are fluent in other languages too – such as hate and prejudice. We've missed something critical here about the work of God's Spirit in our lives if we're happy with this imbalance between outward and inward.

When Paul, the apostle, talked about the type of life that results from following the Holy Spirit's leading in our lives, he doesn't make a list that contains healings, mega-churches, financial security, popularity, health, travel or worship albums... not that there is anything necessarily wrong with these things, but none of this occurs on Paul's itinerary of evidence. His list contains: Love, Joy, Peace, Patience, Kindness, Goodness, Faithfulness, Gentleness and Self-Control[19] – all flavours of character and not the momentary exploits of personalities. If learning is demonstrated through our fruit, and our fruit is a manifestation of our roots (see previous chapter), then surely our *nature* is just as important, if not more important than our *stature*.

Samson is renowned for his strength and abilities – a lifter of gates, a catcher of foxes, a danger with a donkey's jaw bone and a puller-down of strongholds. There are more words written about him and his actions in the book of Judges than any other leader during that period in Israel's history. But a closer inspection of his life would tell us that he wasn't known for love or self-control. In fact, none of his exploits were ever done as an act of loving obedience to God – they were all carried out under Samson's own impulsiveness and concern for self-preservation – it's just that God was able to take these reckless acts and use them to His advantage.

In contrast, Genesis 5:21-24, tells us about a man named Enoch. He walked closely with God. That's all we know about him.

Who was the better student, the one who did great *feats* or the one who *walked*?

I highlight this because we do have this habit of measuring obedience in relation to exploits, but this is an unfair comparison. If the above didn't serve as a clear example, then consider this: Jesus only spent three years doing ministry – does this mean that his previous thirty years were lived in disobedience and were unfruitful?

As a modern example, sadly popular in some modern churches, the person who appears at every official meeting (seven nights a week), who champions the culture of the church, and uses their student loan to tithe into the vision, is seen as a hero. 'They've got it!' we cry, but what about their life outside a formal meeting? Whereas the single parent who's giving everything they have for their children and can only come to a formal meeting once a week is overlooked. Or the employed person, who works crazy hours in a demanding job, but who loves their work colleagues, shows concern for their lives, and gives them assistance whenever they can; they attend church on a regular basis, but have issues/concerns with some of the things that are championed. How are they viewed? Seriously, church leaders out there, who are the heroes? Who are the disciples?

Susanna Wesley once warned her son John that: 'The tree is known by its fruit, but not always by its blossoms. What blossoms beautifully sometimes bears bitter fruit'[20]. Love expressed through learning is not solely concerned with 'how we look', it's more about 'how we taste' – we need to be cautious when we measure our love for God by 'what we are achieving' more than 'who are we becoming'.

So, are we willing to learn from Jesus, through who He is, to become more human, more loving, more joyful, more patient, more kind etc...?

What will you do with that question? Where will you allow it to lead you?

> '...Christ's love controls us. Since we believe that Christ died for all, we also believe that we have all died to our old life. He died for everyone so that those who receive his new life will no longer live for themselves. Instead, they will live for Christ, who died and was raised for them. So we have stopped evaluating others from a human point of view. At one time we thought of Christ merely from a human point of view. How differently we know him now! This means that anyone who belongs to Christ has become a new person. The old life is gone; a new life has begun!' – 2 Corinthians 5:14-17 (NLT)

EXPRESSED THROUGH **MERCY**

'Whenever we are known by love,
God's reputation is intact'
Erwin Raphael McManus[1]

FOSSILS IN THE CUPBOARD

When I was a teenager I did 'my time' as a paper boy with an early morning paper round and, excuse the boast here, I was good at it.

Prior to taking the role on, the round I was given was in a right mess, with customers cancelling their orders each week. The previous paper lad had been consistently late, missed out deliveries on a semi-regular basis – or just got them wrong altogether – and had recently begun to make a habit out of not showing up at all. At least, that's the story I was told.

His last strike was my call – I got in on his failure, which, when looking back, isn't really the best way to proceed. But I was young and eager to prove myself. I'd been grafting away on an evening round for the past year, waiting for an opportunity for the 'big-time' to come up. So I took hold of this opening with everything I had.

Within a matter of weeks I had totally turned the situation around. The existing customers loved me – which expressed itself through the immense amount of tips I got that first Christmas – and through their recommendations their neighbours also wanted to have their papers delivered.

This apparent 'success' caused my boss to declare that I was the best paper boy he'd ever had. And through the ongoing months of maintaining this performance, he grew more and more confident of my abilities – he trusted me – which inevitably led to there being no need to check my papers before I left the shop. Why check someone who doesn't make mistakes?

Sadly though, after two years of being in the star role, I started to abuse this trust.

I'd begun stealing magazines while getting my papers together, knowing the contents of my bag wouldn't be checked. It's not something I'm proud of, and I'm certainly not going to share my technique with you, but I thought I had it down to a tee. My 'skills' had aided me in getting away with a considerable number of issues. And, before you get the wrong picture, I wasn't swiping glossy top-shelf XXX publications (my brothers already had enough of those) – I was pilfering palaeontology! (Magazines about dinosaurs, to be more specific).

However, it turned out my technique wasn't as good as I thought – as one Saturday morning, while getting my papers together, and after five minutes of thinking that I had executed another perfect swipe, Mr Singh (the newsagent) said, 'Tristan, you're next to be checked'.

I went numb.

I knew I'd been spotted – there was no other reason he would have asked. My hands got sweaty, the adrenaline flowed, the colour drained from my face. This strange feeling came over me – fear, guilt, shame – not any one of those in isolation, but a concoction of them all in one swift dose. Have you ever felt like this – knowing you'd been caught and then finding yourself waiting for judgement to be passed, uncertain of what the reaction would be?

I wasn't caught yet though. Maybe it was coincidence, just a routine thing. Maybe another paper boy had complained about how unfair it was that my papers never got checked, and maybe as an attempt to 'cool' the issue Mr Singh had agreed to do one? With that in mind, I tried to perform my procedure in reverse and return the magazine. But, in the midst of the attempt I was met with 'Don't bother trying to do that Tristan, I've already seen it. Just bring all your papers up here'.

Yep, I'd been caught.

So, in a cold sweat, I carried my pile of papers over to the shop counter. And, even though he knew the magazine was in there, and even though he knew that I knew he knew it was in there, he made me check through each paper in turn until finally the magazine on fossils exposed itself, mid-stack, sandwiched between a 'broadsheet' and a 'tabloid'.

Caught red-handed.

I tried making some excuse, acting surprised to find it myself – 'I must have accidentally picked it up with *The Guardian*, thinking it was a supplement...' But no, he'd witnessed me doing this once before, and he'd spotted regular problems in his stock checks.

At this point I could feel the attention of everyone else in the shop fixing itself firmly on the events that were unfolding. As a paper boy I earned a living through pushing the scandals of others through people's letter boxes, I wasn't prepared for myself being the breaking news that day.

It's hard to describe how I felt. This man trusted me, and I had stolen from him – worse, I had used (maybe this would be better termed 'ab-used') the context of this trust as a means to steal. I could only stand there and agree with all he had to say as he questioned and lectured me – there was no defence or excuse for my actions. While he interrogated me externally, internally I was chastising myself, 'Why did I do this?', 'Were these magazines worth this – are they worth losing your job and reputation for?'

It was a weird awakening. It's not like I'd only just discovered that what I was doing was wrong, immoral, damaging – I always knew – but somehow, in my desire for a few scattered facts about an Apatosaurus and the model parts to build my own T-Rex, I had managed to cut off those feelings. It's scary to think that we're able to cut off the warning signals just like that. The spotlight had found me and not only exposed my true nature to my boss, but also to myself.

Eventually, the trial ended and Mr Singh readied himself to deliver his verdict – 'So what should I do with you?' They're the kind of words that linger in your consciousness more than they do in actual time. What would he do? After all, I'd stolen over one hundred pounds worth of merchandise! He continued, 'I'm not going to fire you, *but*, your papers will be checked every day from now on. And I don't want to catch you doing this again'.

What? It was hard to take in. I stood there speechless, feeling paralysed by this man's response. I deserved to lose my job, there was absolutely no doubt of that, but Mr Singh had instead chosen to be merciful. I can't really remember giving a response, although I think I may have nodded an acknowledgement of sorts with a stunned look on my face – stunned because of the freedom that had just been graciously returned to me.

He didn't even ask me to pay anything back.

As I left the shop that morning, I did so in two minds about myself – I felt dirty, rotten, horrible about what I had done, but I also felt strangely clean. I had been caught, but also set free.

Looking back after all these years, this experience still remains a powerful one for me. This exposure to mercy changed me.

I'm sure I'm not the only one who has ever been caught. And I'm sure most of us have either experienced first-hand, or heard about through others, the damage or manipulation people can inflict when our scandals are revealed – when others use an individual's shame or failure as leverage to humiliate and dehumanise, instead of to recover and restore.

My boss could have destroyed me, or demeaned me, or even used the incident as a means for worse things – but that wasn't his character. His character was marked by compassion, and this expression of care caused me to realise my ways and change. I have many regrets in life, and I do most certainly regret stealing, but I don't regret getting caught. Getting caught was one of the best things that happened to me – it led me to experience the new life that results from an expression of love called mercy.

It takes a lot of effort to keep the fossils hidden, from others and even to ourselves, but when exposed – and exposed in the right environment – then there is freedom to be found and a new lease of life to live.

EXPOSED

Jesus told a similar story, the story of a king who one day decided to bring all his accounts up to date. Eugene Peterson, author of *The Message*, paraphrases the story like this:

> *"The kingdom of God is like a king who decided to square accounts with his servants. As he got under way, one servant was brought before him who had run up a debt of a hundred thousand dollars. He couldn't pay up, so the king ordered the man, along with his wife, children, and goods, to be auctioned off at the slave market.*
>
> *"The poor wretch threw himself at the king's feet and begged, 'Give me a chance and I'll pay it all back.' Touched by his plea, the king let him off, erasing the debt.*
>
> *"The servant was no sooner out of the room when he came upon one of his fellow servants who owed him ten dollars. He seized him by the throat and demanded, 'Pay up. Now!'*
>
> *"The poor wretch threw himself down and begged, 'Give me a chance and I'll pay it all back.' But he wouldn't do it. He had him arrested and put in jail until the debt*

was paid. When the other servants saw this going on, they were outraged and brought a detailed report to the king.

"The king summoned the man and said, 'You evil servant! I forgave your entire debt when you begged me for mercy. Shouldn't you be compelled to be merciful to your fellow servant who asked for mercy?' The king was furious and put the screws to the man until he paid back his entire debt. And that's exactly what my Father in heaven is going to do to each one of you who doesn't forgive unconditionally anyone who asks for mercy"[2].

It's a story that is both beautiful and horrific.

Beautiful – because, a man doesn't get what he does deserve (*mercy*) and instead is given what he doesn't deserve (*grace*), which should, in turn, bring about a sudden expansion (if not birth) to a whole dimension of freedom within his reality.

To see this, you'll have to place yourself in this man's shoes for a moment.

This man would have known he was heavily in debt, it's not something that is easy to forget, and this knowledge would have had a massive influence over his life – what he would do, where he would go, who he would see – all these choices would have been made with the weight of this huge sum brooding at the forefront of his mind. His sense of direction each day would have been tormented by the amount of money he owed.

And it was a huge figure!

Jesus suggests a ridiculous sum of money, it's like saying 'infinity', but that's the idea of the story – it's an unpayable amount, regardless of the extent of effort that is exercised to pay it off. Whatever this man manages to gather in a day would barely scratch the surface – he cannot earn his way out of this, work won't save him. You have to try and picture the amount of anxiety this must have caused – maybe for some of us we've shared this reality ourselves. This figure would eclipse your world, overshadowing and tainting everything. It would rob you of sleep. It would chip away at your identity. It would also steal from you the ability of seeing life in colour.

I use that last statement because, as someone who has had struggles with depression and anxiety, I can say that I have often described life, or my own feelings about life, as being 'grey'. There may have been contrasts in the things I saw, better moments than others, but those contrasts were normally differences in hue – light grey to dark grey. At least having the 'blues' is fortunate to have some kind of tone to it.

It's important that we feel this man's predicament. It would be unwise to hit these stories with our moral compasses at the ready, looking to see who the bad guy is and who's the good guy – who's wearing black and who's wearing white. We can make a nasty habit of reading the whole story and then stepping back to ask "who do we align ourselves with" (or for some people, who represents "us", and who represents "them"). But let's hold back on our judgements, and instead journey with the man through the story – let's not condemn the man at the start because of what we discover at the end – he's not the bad guy, he's just broken! Broken in a way that found resonance within the people who heard this story for the first time, and broken in a way that still continues to find an echo within our own time.

While we're talking about bad-guys vs good-guys, please understand that the king isn't the villain either – don't imagine him sat on his throne in some secret lair, stroking a white cat[3] while surrounded by an army of expendable henchmen.

This king has generously furnished this servant's life, he has loaned him money time, after time, after time. How often isn't stated, but it's unlikely the man borrowed all that he owed within a single transaction. And he's just *a* servant, one from all the other servants the king has aided. It makes sense that at some point the king will have to carry out a stock check, especially if he desires to continue providing support.

In short, the first part of the story could be broken down like this – it's about a man in debt, a King who desires reconciliation and an imbalance that cannot be ignored.

Eventually the day comes when the man has to face what he has feared – he is brought before the throne. His debt is revealed and the consequences of his actions suddenly burst into view, threatening to engulf not only himself, but also his family.

He's exposed.

But concealed within that exposure are also the origins of his rebirth. After pleading with the king, the man is forgiven – the king chooses to absorb the huge debt that is owed, paying the price himself, and then releases his servant.

Which should cause a bigger 'What?' than my response to Mr Singh.

This story doesn't meet with our expectations, hence its beauty – this is a highly attractive resolution, one that I suspect many of us dream of.

Imagine being the man at that moment.

Can you conceive how this would feel – to have the thing that has caused such anxiety, such depression, such fear, suddenly lifted from you? No more decisions being made under the shadow of his debt. He's no longer a slave to his circumstances.

Imagine that release.

Imagine the man's heart beating in his chest as he hears 'You don't have to pay anything back, it's cleared. You're free. Go'.

He's just been sentenced, not *for* life, but *to* life!

Again, it's a beautiful story.

No longer does the activity of his days need to be defined by the debt he once owed.

And yet tragically, within that freedom, within that life, the man chooses not to express that which he has received – he makes the choice to allow his expression speak of his old life, and not of his new identity. He goes on to live like a man judged, and not as a man forgiven – but we'll come back to this later, because we also have to recognise that this story is horrific, and not because of the tragedy just mentioned. It's scarier for a far deeper reason, and one that might already be apparent to you – to have been shown mercy involved the man being exposed.

And none of us long for that, or do we?

We have a TV show in the UK called *'Embarrassing Bodies'* – it's not the kind of television show you can watch while eating a kebab! The concept is simple enough – people come and expose their ailments to expert medical practitioners, not because they're exhibitionists (I think?), but as a means of finally discovering a cure for their illness. Needless to say, most of the conditions that the show reveals are fairly shocking, but the ones that take my breath away aren't what you would expect. It's not the misdiagnoses from GPs, or the mutilations that were intended to be cosmetic/reconstructive surgeries. It's the cases like this: when what began as a small open sore on an ankle has been allowed twelve months to develop across most of the bottom half of a leg, becoming infected and gangrenous, and yet those afflicted never once sought medical advice. And in not seeking, they in turn condemned themselves to more ill health and damage, allowing the rate of decay to accelerate.

The thing is, these people are not stupid, they aren't crazy – they're simply embarrassed (hence the title of the show). Getting help means exposure, but there exists within them this awareness of the damage that human society can inflict on the one who is exposed. It's heartbreaking to witness the extent to which a problem has to grow before we are compelled to step out of the shadows and say, 'Help!'

Health
    Debt
        Addiction
            Depression
                Sin

Just to name a few. We want aid, or sometimes just simply acknowledgement that we are not alone in our struggle, but we're aware that we can often become targets for shame, prejudice, hate, anger or maybe even exile. We long for redemption, but we fear exposure. We long to feel clean, we desire wholeness, but we feel that no place exists where we can expose ourselves in order to feel the release and freedom that mercy brings with it. So we carry our burdens, allowing their infection to spread deeper and further...

Embarrassed

Ashamed

Guilty

Afraid

I find it interesting in this story that this man doesn't go to the king first, he would rather wait until he's summoned. He's been to the king for help before, and received it, why not now? Did he feel he had exhausted the king's goodness and generosity? Was he simply embarrassed at having to ask again? Whatever his reasons, he had chosen to wait until the problem would expose itself. Maybe it's easier that way, especially when each day promises to be a trial but never a sentencing.

This may seem like a strange thing to say, but I wonder if he longed for judgment? At least judgement changes the scene – it moves the story forward, it offers some form of release from our current plight, even if that release comes in the form of punishment. Maybe some of us want to be caught – we feel we cannot tell, we cannot expose ourselves, but at least being discovered says it for us? Even then we still fear the reaction.

We feel ugly, or are made to feel ugly, so we expect ugly.

We long for a place of refuge, but many of us suspect that what we'll walk into will be a slaughterhouse.

In the story Jesus told, the man discovers that it's in the presence of the king, the place he had expected to find condemnation, where he finds compassion – he finds sanctuary.

SANCTUARY

Mercy provides the sanctuary we all desire, but such an environment can only exist if the architect is love.

When mercy is unleashed it seeks not to destroy *or* to keep hidden, but to recover and to restore. An environment that cultivates mercy is one where exposure feels both safe and natural, not because of some exhibitionist urge, but because there is a desire from all those who gather in such communities for healing, wholeness, transformation and release. It's imperative that love is the central expression of these communities, a love for each other, a love that doesn't see 'good guys' or 'bad guys', but recognises that we're all broken, all in need of repair and renovation.

That's why groups such as 'Alcoholics Anonymous' are so powerful. With one voice people declare their issue, 'I'm a ....', and find themselves in a community that not only supports them, but sees them and identifies *with* them. They find acceptance, not of their problem, but of their identity as a human being, a human being who needs help in their struggle to live.

I'm a sinner

That's not a statement about my past. It's a statement that speaks of Jesus' righteousness, and not my own. I have this pre-disposition to mess-up, to make bad choices, to fail. It's only by the grace and mercy of God that I live.

I am a sinner.

We all are.

I'm not alone. You're not alone. We're *all* broken. And it's not a measure of who is more disfigured, it's not about the extent of our fractures – we have *all* fallen short of the glory of God, but on the cross God decided to absorb the debt of all this brokenness. His body was broken for you, for me – for us. At the cross, the throne of the King of kings, we are summoned to receive our sentence, and with the resurrection we receive our commission to live.

As my Pastor used to say, 'God has enough on all of us to bury us', but the offer of new life comes to us regardless of who we are or what we have done[4]. Jesus offers us His beauty where we would expect to receive brutality – '...*for he faced all of the same testings we do, yet he did not sin. So let us come boldly to the throne of our gracious God. There we will receive his mercy, and we will find grace to help us when we need it most*'[5].

As a follower of Christ, I realise that when I come before this throne, that I am not the only one – I am part of a community of people who seek and require the mercy that flows from this seat on a daily basis. None of us have been invited into the king's presence to receive applause, or accolades and tributes – we have all been extended an invitation of grace to come and receive love and compassion and new life.

Yet, we can forget this basis of our calling, and we can forget the purpose of this sanctuary. If we forget that it is love that has called us to this place, love that has received us, love that sits enthroned on the mercy seat, then the sanctuary will degrade into a pool called Bethesda. A place where broken people will gather in competition with each other, and where the only changes that transpire result from either the continual hunger of atrophy, or through the damage inflicted to those caught in the crush of others desperately seeking their own honour.

The sanctuary exists not to imprison us, but to release us. It's not designed with the purpose that we gather together and watch each other decay – this refuge exists with the purpose to form us, and mould us. After all, the Kingdom of God, the rule of Christ, is a Kingdom of Resurrection.

We are sentenced to live.

> '*Do not let sin control the way you live... Instead give yourselves completely to God since you have been given*

new life. And use your whole body as a tool to do what is right for the glory of God'[6]

We leave His throne room debt free, but still in debt.

'Pay all your debts, except the debt of love for others. You can never finish paying that!'[7]

Therefore the challenge, the ruling we should pass over each other's lives is the same as the one we have received – I sentence you to live, and live in honour of the King who has granted us life!

Within the parable that Jesus told, there is an expectation that we automatically place on the man when he leaves the throne room of the king. It may be one that is left unsaid, but it's one that we naturally hear (and one that is confirmed at the end of the story). The king expects the man to express the love/mercy that he has been shown; he is expected to become an active part in the expansion of the agenda that he has just benefited from – he is called to be an expression of the king.

But this fails to be realised.

In life, like in this story, the problems begin to kick in when we leave the sanctuary, or when we fail to grasp what just took place there.

'BUT WHEN THE MAN LEFT THE KING....'

To sense that something has gone drastically wrong in the second part of the story is to be aware of the great gift that this man has just been given. What went wrong and why so soon?

The story presents us with a few little twists and revelations to help us on our way.

The first thing that comes to the forefront is quite ironic – we discover that the man in debt was also a moneylender. The man with the large loan was a loan shark. Think about this for a second. His life's foundation was built upon taking what belonged to his master and giving it to others – as long as it had some eventual return to himself. But, when shown mercy, he struggles to pass this on to his cliental – there's no business sense in that transaction. To live to the king's agenda would mean death to his own – he cannot expand his own empire using his master's business ethic.

The second thing that stands out is the man's actions. He seems more aggressive and impatient in his approach than the king did. For example, he grabs his fellow servant by the throat. It's a pretty clear gesture, one that says 'I have no interest in what you have to say' – he removes his fellow servant's right to speak. And then, when his fellow servant does eventually receive the space to take a breath and plead for the time to pay (using more or less the same words as his persecutor had used moments before), the request falls on deaf ears (or a dull heart) and he's imprisoned. The first man totally fails to see what is clear to us as observers to this (and to the observers in the story) – he's blind to the reflection of this man's condition before himself, and his own condition before the king just a few moments earlier.

The first man wanted the king to understand his difficulties, his inabilities, the things preventing him doing what he should have done, but when it came to expressing what he had received – he can't even be bothered to hear his fellow servant's story. He doesn't care about the other servant's problems, reasons or restrictions. He has no love for this other man, and no interest in seeing something develop in his life. So much so, that he restricts this man's growth, by placing him in a "prison". In a nutshell, he's happy to be in process, but he's not willing to accept that others are also.

After what happened to him in the throne room how can he react in such a way? Does he somehow believe that he'd earned the mercy he was shown?

There is a key ingredient missing here between his response and the king's, one I feel that the storyteller purposely highlights by not mentioning it within the second part of this tale – *pity/compassion* (or *touched*, in Eugene Peterson's version). The Greek word used is *splanchnizomai* – which is a description of being moved in the 'splanchna' (the 'splanchna' being a description of our internal organs, the guts in particular).[8] In modern times the heart has become the international symbol of love and its source, but in ancient times love's centre was the stomach. I suppose for both ancient and modern the intended meaning is the same, regardless of whether our 'stomachs churn' or our 'hearts go out' – we're describing the echo we feel when we find a resonance with the depths of another. However, I do prefer the image of the guts, it prevents us from turning the definition of love into some gushy romantic feeling – this kind of love causes a bowel movement!

A powerful inner movement that *recognises* ourselves in the faces of those that sit before us.

A reflection that connects in such a way, that we're able to *feel* the plight of others and imagine ourselves in their condition.

A sensitivity that leads us to the *understanding* that the person before us is more than their current set of circumstances.

An awareness that desires to see people *released* to be all they are made to be, and not restricted.

Love is what births mercy because, as Viktor E. Frankl beautifully put it:

> *'Love is the only way to grasp another human being in the innermost core of his personality. No one can become fully aware of the very essence of another human being unless he loves him. By his love he is enabled to see the essential traits and features in the beloved person; and even more, he sees that which is potential in him, which is not yet actualized but yet ought to be actualized. Furthermore, by his love, the*

loving person enables the beloved person to actualise these potentialities. By making him aware of what he can be and what he should become, he makes these potentialities come true'[9]

Love – the king had it, but servant number one lacked it. After being the recipient of such grace and mercy this lack is unexplainable, and seems ridiculous – but maybe that's the point of the story.

Surely those who are shown much love, go on to show much love[10]?

Don't they?

Sadly, not always.

If we fail to see and appreciate what transpired when we found ourselves in the sanctuary, we will struggle to invite others into it. We cannot express what we haven't really received.

Love expresses itself to us through the demonstration of mercy, but also, our expression of love is shown through our reception of it.

Do we see mercy as just being let off the hook, a divine consent to pursue our own agenda, or do we see it as a call to repentance – when we put down our agendas and begin to reciprocate the agenda that has liberated us?

SWEAT PANTS

A few years ago I decided it was about time that I made some effort to get healthier. In my early twenties I used jog on a fairly regular basis each morning – nothing in the way of a marathon, but just enough to get the heart pumping – until one autumn evening, when I partially tore a ligament in my right foot by simply walking down some steps. The healing process didn't really complete until early December, at which point I seriously lacked the motivation to begin the jogging process again on cold, wet, dark winter mornings. I "reasoned" that it would be best to wait for spring before starting over. Spring came, and then summer, then the year after that and so on. Then the dynamics of life really shifted; Steph and I had kids, I got more involved in leading church, my responsibilities at work began increasing etc... I spent a large quantity of time running about but not in a healthy way. As I approached my thirties, I was feeling 'the burn' just walking up the stairs. It was time for change.

But, you can't just rush into these things. I'd been out of the jogging game for a while – I at least needed some new gear. So, as well as a fresh pair of trainers ('trainees' in my native accent), I also felt it necessary to purchase some new training pants.

I should explain here, that when I say training pants, I mean 'jogging bottoms', 'sweatpants' – not nappies!

The right pants are essential – you can't jog in jeans. You need something comfortable, movement-friendly, non-chafing – preferably with an elasticated waist.

I honestly bought all this stuff with the best intention to start over, but I never really took up jogging again – but I still found a use for the trousers. After a tough day at work I come home, spend some time with the family, put the kids to bed, and get ready to relax by throwing off the work clothes and getting changed into my "slob-pants" (as Steph has aptly re-branded them).

It's ironic that I can take something which has been designed for the pursuit of fitness, something whose purpose is to aid me on my journey to a healthier me, and totally abuse its function so that it actually becomes a comforter to my laziness, complacency and inadequacy.

But I wouldn't be the first one to do this, would I?

It seems to be an issue in humanity as a whole – we have a track record for taking that which is meant for good, and using it to bring harm.

Take *Facebook* and other social media for instance. They are powerful and fantastic tools. Because of the rise in social media, a revolution in how we do relationships has taken place just in the space of a decade. Phone applications and online communities are useful ways to keep connected, share news and discover people. But, we're all aware that there exist *those people* who take what is designed to connect people, and use it to damage people. I'm sure most of us have witnessed *Facebook* being used as a place to rant about others, complain, verbally abuse, slander, bully, pick fights and disclose things that should have been kept in confidence. (Just in case you feel I might be targeting certain individuals here – we're all capable of being *those people*).

3D Printing is the kind of future technology that I dreamed of as a kid. To think that it now exists in my time, along with touchscreen mobile technology and actual, real-looking computer generated images in films (I can see myself eventually eating my words on that last one) – what's next, *Hover-boards* and *Self-drying Jackets*?[11] Only the other day I was reading on the *BBC News* website about how they're now using 3D printing technology to form parts that can be used in reconstructive surgery and for creating personalised equipment for those with disabilities – that's an amazing use of technology! But, what was one of the most popular and controversial designs to be downloaded for this technology?

From nuclear fission and pharmaceuticals, to food and money, even an individual's trust – humanity's ability to take what can be used for good and then use it to bring harm, certainly speaks of how far we've fallen from reflecting an image of the divine[12].

And then there's *Mercy*.

I've come to believe and experience the powerful expression of love that is mercy. Mercy is something that God Himself uses in His dealings within the lives of humanity, to shape and mould us into the people that we are designed to be. Through the expression of His love, God uses mercy to form us, not destroy us; He doesn't beat us into shape, he loves us into it.

However, like all good innovations, both the use and the reception of mercy by humanity can degrade it to become a means to inflict wounds and excuse the lack of change. If not careful, mercy can become just a pair of "spiritual slob pants".

To see this, we only need to take a quick scan through the story of the Old Testament.

BARKING MAD

The Old Testament gives us an amazing picture of how God's mercy operates. If you've ever read any of the books of the Prophets it's easy to misinterpret God as being an angry, grumpy, wrathful deity, whose emotional state can change with a flick of a switch. But when you read the Prophets, you really have to understand them in their historical context.

I'm not going to give a full run through of that history, but I would encourage you to consider the times and socio-political circumstances described in the books of 1 and 2 Kings the next time you find yourself reading the words of Isaiah, Jeremiah etc...

In short, Israel was the nation that God had chosen through grace, a nation he called His 'special possession', to express His nature to the rest of humanity. Even if you know only a little of the Old Testament, then I suspect that you're already aware that they (like ourselves) struggled in this expression.

But God doesn't throw them, or the people He calls, away when they fail in being all He has called them to be. As the writer of *Samuel* tells us:

> 'God does not just sweep life away; instead, he devises ways to bring us back when we have been separated from him.'[13]

God's love for Israel meant that He was faithful to them and because of this faithfulness to His people, when they did wrong, He would bring His word to them. His mercy towards them meant that He warned them of the consequences and self-destruction that would result from their actions. The Prophets then, were an expression of God's mercy to His people – they carried His words and spoke them into the nation/s about them, speaking of the need for change in order to avoid disaster.

At no point through this process does God desire His people to experience the fallout of their choices. He isn't sadistically brooding over the world waiting to unleash destruction and punishment – actually, the only reference that comes to mind of God brooding over something is at the start of *Genesis*, as His Spirit broods and hovers over the waters of a formless earth, desiring and dreaming about the creation of life to come – a desire that moves God to be vocal.

God loves, God longs for life, and so God speaks.

But then God would do something interesting with His wayward people – He would bring His word, and then He would step back, waiting for the people to repent/change, giving them more warnings if needed and allowing them the time to work through this change process for themselves. Again and again through the prophets, God appeals to His people to come back into the sanctuary of their covenant relationship with Him, and begin once again to allow that sanctuary to find expression in their lives.

In short, God's mercy was expressed through His words and also through His provision of time to allow change to take place. He encourages *and* He empowers them to change. And He appears to be lavish in this – never really allowing the fullness of the consequences, or His discipline, to be rolled out.

I've been told this is bad parenting. That if you make a threat, then you should carry it out – there's plenty of bark, but never any bite. But it appears that God always prefers to see change over calamity. He would rather *form* us through the reception of His lavish love for us, than *beat* us into shape through His wrath.

I have to ask – and please be honest here – if you were a citizen of any of these times, and a person claiming to speak for God showed up and called you to change in order to avoid the damage your lifestyle choices were inflicting on yourself and society as a whole, and then they began to graphically describe the fallout that would follow if you kept pursuing your current course, but then those consequences never came, what would you think?

If it was me, I'd think the prophet was a liar, or just plain barking mad.

And so the people the prophets spoke to, naturally (for want of a much better word) see this lack of discipline/consequence as proof that the prophet was wrong and they were right. So the change never happens, or at the most, it only lasts for a season.

I wonder, is this what happens in the parable? I'm sure the man was grateful for what had happened, I'm sure he feels less burdened, but he never fully realises why he was invited into the sanctuary.

Does he leave the King feeling vindicated, instead of forgiven?

Do we sometimes view God's grace as Him being pro *our* agenda, when actually God's acting because He's pro His *own* agenda?

This is the misuse of mercy. This is when we begin to take the King's acts of grace and mercy and wear them like "slob pants", when we mistake God's forgiveness as our vindication. Where, instead of being[14] transformed through the continual experience of His love, we use His love to comfort ourselves in our complacency.

THE LAST WORD

In the Old Testament story, despite God's lavish expression of language and time, there comes the point when, like the king in the parable, God summons the people of Israel to account.

After thousands of words, through a large host of prophets speaking over five hundred plus years, God lets the consequences come, and Israel are taken from the land that He had given them. This is hardly the picture of a God whose emotions turn at the drop of a hat.

It's during this time that the prophet Jeremiah, while reflecting and lamenting on the destruction of Jerusalem and the exile of his people, poetically expresses the following:

> '*The faithful love of the Lord never ends! His mercies never cease. Great is his faithfulness his mercies begin afresh each day*'[15]

Jeremiah's wandering abandoned streets. He's weeping over the carcasses of buildings. He's wailing about the hundreds of missing faces who used to walk those same lanes and fill those market squares, but who are now either in captivity or are left behind, abandoned to desolation. And Jeremiah makes a statement like this!

Even in the midst of the fallout around him, Jeremiah can still see the mercy of God in action – even in the midst of catastrophe he recognises that God's purpose is not to abandon them. Even in this God is still forming them. God's mercy is still working away within this exposure, cultivating an origin for freedom. God keeps on speaking, He keeps on loving His people and He continues calling them to 'choose life'. From Jeremiah's perspective, God's last word was not in his day.

I love this verse in Lamentations. I don't know about you, but I am extremely grateful that God's mercies are new every day – I need them each day. If we understand the context here then we'll see how humbling this is, as it speaks of God's daily goodness overriding and working out through our daily failures.

Echoing the words of prophets like Samuel and Jeremiah, Nadia Bolz-Weber puts the beauty of God's mercy like this:

> 'God simply keeps reaching down into the dirt of humanity and resurrecting us from the graves we dig for ourselves through our violence, our lies, our selfishness, our arrogance, and our addictions. And God keeps loving us back to life over and over'[16]

The writer of the New Testament letter *Hebrews* says that '*Long ago God spoke many times and in many ways to our ancestors through the prophets. But now in these final days, he has spoken to us through his Son*'[17]. God's final (yet eternal) word to us, is Jesus. If you ever wanted to know what God has to say to us, well, Jesus is His answer. His death communicates to us all that we need to know about His compassion for us – that, even when the full consequences of our choices come to engulf us, it's God Who places Himself between us and flood waters.

He dies, in order that we might live.

He's forsaken, while we're forgiven.

He's broken, so that we can be redeemed and repaired.

He's restricted, and nailed, and condemned, allowing us to have the freedom to choose life, and become all that He has called us to be.

His death tears open a way to the sanctuary.

Love, expressed through mercy, demonstrated through the bloodied nail-pierced hands of the One who refuses to let us go.

I love this lavish, faithful love of God. But, can I be honest? I also find it challenging and exhausting. There are times when I like being who I am right now; times, when I just want to pull on my 'slob-pants', and coast through this journey of faith; times, when I don't want to change my opinion, when I cling to the past, when I hold on to my own badly-constructed theology. There are even moments when I, like the man in the story, don't want to forget the debt I am owed, regardless of the fact that it no longer defines my identity.

There are seasons when I want God to just sign my sick note, but God's mercy persists. He didn't die to issue me a licence, but to liberate me.

Here's how it is – none of us ever graduate from the sanctuary, none of us can ever dispose of our need for mercy.

CLAY

As I said in the previous chapter, we have been called on a journey of discipleship to Jesus, a journey that takes time, a journey that will be full of ups and downs, times when we get it right and times when we blow it big time. There is an image God wishes to reform in us, not beat into us, and His love expressed through mercy is the primary instrument in crafting that shape, and the sanctuary is His workshop.

This is stressed in the way that God talks about His relationship with humanity, as He describes Himself as a potter and not a blacksmith.

In Jeremiah 18:3-4, God gives the 'weeping prophet' a picture of His divine nature by asking Jeremiah to observe a potter creating a jar out of clay. God shows Jeremiah that when a fault begins to develop in the pot, then the potter will take it back down to a lump and begin to reshape it. The artisan doesn't throw the material away, he simply recognises it could be so much more, and so persists with the clay until it reaches the extent of the potter's imagination. This is the process of mercy.

I hope we all deeply desire to see the hands of God working on each of our lives, shaping us, forming us, moulding us into something beautiful. The question is, do we trust the design God has for our own life, and for each other's lives? And do we trust Him enough to allow Him the time to do what He needs to do?

I long for sanctuary. My dream is that church can be the place where people can be open and honest about their difficulties and struggles and receive mercy; that church can provide the space and time where people find resonance for the purpose of renovation and resurrection; where everybody is welcome, because everyone is broken, and where healing actually takes place via the medium of love. I don't long for pools like Bethesda.

The thing is, church isn't a place, it's communities of people who have been impacted by the King's generosity, and called to share that generosity. Which leads to a scary truth – sometimes I will experience God's mercy directly from His throne, but for the rest of the time I depend on it indirectly through the prophetic lives of others, and others depend on it indirectly through me.

This means our discipleship is not an individualistic pursuit – it needs all of us together. I need your words and time, and you need mine – as long as those expressions are an expansion of the King's agenda, an echo of what we have received. This journey of learning is a long process, so we have to be open to sharing and receiving direction, guidance, encouragement and buckets full of grace.

God's shaping me and God's shaping you, so while we're all still on the potter's wheel, let's learn to receive and express love through mercy.

> 'You didn't think, did you, that just by pointing your finger at others you would distract God from seeing all your misdoings and from coming down on you hard? Or did you think that because he's such a nice God, he'd let you off the hook? Better think this one through from the beginning. God is kind, but he's not soft. In kindness he takes us firmly by the hand and leads us into a radical life-change' – Romans 2:3-4 (The Message)

> 'For you have been called to live in freedom, my brothers and sisters. But don't use your freedom to satisfy your sinful nature. Instead, use your freedom to serve one another in love' – Galatians 5:13 (NLT)

EXPRESSED THROUGH **SERVICE**

'People are strange, when you're a stranger'
THE DOORS[1]

BIRTH

When Steph and I were expectant parents, we did our time watching those infamous TV documentaries that capture the whole miraculous event of birth – you know the ones I'm talking about? The documentaries where easy births never seem to be given any air time.

Agreed, *birth* and *easy* shouldn't be allowed to sit together in the same sentence, but the deliveries these programmes showcased always had to be the ones that involved narrations like, 'Sharon has now been in labour for seventy-two hours...' coupled with 'even after having the epidural, she is still in tremendous pain'. As we watched, the distance between us on the sofa would always close up, not out of some romantic attraction, but just out of sheer concern – this stuff was terrifying. I honestly don't know why we kept tuning in, these shows never really helped to instil any positive anticipation of the upcoming event, but we were hooked. Ironically, the amount of time we spent watching those shows totalled more time than both our births put together. And yet, despite all of this exposure, at every conceivable camera angle, nothing really prepared us for the multi-faceted, emotion-fuelled metamorphosis of bump to baby.

Birth is beautiful, but very sweaty. It is breathtaking, but exhausting. It's both divine and fleshy. It's enthralling, gritty, joyful, messy, painful, thrilling, good, peaceful and noisy. The whole process of birth bombards your senses with messages that require responses; you cannot sit idly by – birth doesn't seek to entertain but invites you to engage. Regardless of how good the definition is on your TV, you can never really know this sensory demand unless you are physically present as the process unfolds.

That's often the limitation with TV – it allows us to watch from a safe distance, but we cannot participate, we observe but we don't experience. It's this lack of experience, this inability to respond, that in turn forces us to acknowledge that our actions are unable to affect the circumstances unfolding before our eyes; we are left with no choice but to resign our responsibility to act. The space between us and them, or us and that, or us and there, is too great to overcome. I'm not anti-television, but sometimes I wonder whether all this *seeing* with a consistent denial to my senses to respond has caused something within me to become numb? Could it be that I (or we?) have become so used to the *distance* that TV creates that we find it almost natural to virtually impose this space even when it no longer exists?[2]

But back to birth... or more specifically, a birth.

Our second son was born near the end of August 2008. Steph and I had both been hoping that 'little man no.2' would be an early arrival, we even tried a few old-wives methods in the hope that we could negotiate this a little. One of those methodologies must have paid off, but the definition of early that we got didn't quite match with what I had in mind (I still put it down to the curry!).

It was four o'clock in the morning when Steph woke me with the words, 'It's time'. I remember looking at the clock and mumbling into the pillow, 'For what'? It certainly wasn't time for work! At four in the morning an energy-saving light bulb has a quicker response time that my brain does, so before I would be willing to resist the comfort of my duvet I was in need of a little contextualisation. Steph very willingly, voluntarily and 'gently' provided this. With a sense of urgency, and a fear of my wife, now deeply instilled in me the preparations began.

Following the relative smoothness of our first son's birth, we had decided on a home birth this time around. The principle is much the same as a hospital birth, with the exception that when it's time, you don't go to them, they come to you – I suppose you could compare the convenience of the process to a takeaway, but I wouldn't take that analogy too far. Without the unnecessary hassle of travel involved, preparations would be a lot simpler than previously; prepare the bed, get some towels ready, hook my wife up to the TENS machine (should that be the other way round?), ring the mother-in-law, put the kettle on, and wait. But we never got to the wait stage, or the kettle stage for that matter. Within fifteen minutes of us both being awake, Steph's contractions had accelerated from an 'occasional dull ache' to 'hitting hard every minute!' It was time to phone in the order. I figured that at four o'clock in the morning the journey from the hospital to our house shouldn't take any longer than ten minutes, so there's no need for panic, what could possibly go wrong?

Twenty minutes on from the phone call and things are really happening; our son had continued to keep his foot firmly pressed against his mother's biological 'pedal'. Steph was not looking her comfortable best at this point; we'd hit the sweaty stage, the TENS machine was on its highest possible setting, and Steph – between deep breaths – was telling me that she really felt the need to push.

This is fine, this is normal, this is the process of birth – these are the things that need to happen. It's just that I would have preferred them to be taking place with a midwife in the room!

Now it was time for panic.

I've seen this kind of thing take place in films, except that there's usually some calm and collected stranger willing to just step in and save the day, but there's just myself, my wife and our sleeping seventeen-month old son in the neighbouring room. With the inevitable looming and panic starting to set in, I quickly picked up the phone and called the midwife team again to try and find out what was happening.

'I'm really sorry Mr Sherwin, the midwife has had some car trouble, but don't worry...' responds the lady on the phone, *'she's on her way now, we've also dispatched an emergency paramedic to you, and I'm going to remain on the phone with you'.*

I didn't really need to ask why she felt the need to *'remain on the phone'*, my imagination (or paranoia) had already jumped ahead of the events, but her next words really brought it home; *'You'll have to do this Mr Sherwin, but I'll be here to guide you through it'.*

How could I refuse?

Seriously, that's what I was thinking – 'How?' What excuse could possibly work in a moment like this to decline the responsibility that was being given to me? I'm not a midwife, I wasn't trained for this; the closest I'd ever come to birth was dissecting a bull's eyeball at secondary school.

I couldn't refuse or delegate this to the next passer-by, despite how much I would have liked to. Again, my mind begins to drift to media references about people in the midst of crises feeling some 'call', some greatness, suddenly awaken within them – but for me, that awakening never came. Confidence didn't suddenly burst forth; my inadequacy continued casting its large shadow. But I couldn't just sit back and do nothing either, I had to get involved. The predicament was a difficult one, but the choice wasn't.

You see, I love my wife! Because of love I must serve her. By *love* I don't mean some sloppy romantic compulsion; I would never describe myself as a romantic, especially when woken up at four in the morning. Steph was hardly at her most alluring at this point, and childbirth is certainly not some picturesque scene like a candlelit dinner or a beautiful sunset. But my love for Steph was saying, 'You can't walk away from this, you have a duty here'.

It's in moments like these, when those around us are exposed and their need is clearly perceived, that love works on us to unlearn the nurtured numbness between *sensing* and *responding*. It isn't bravery or confidence that needs to rise within us when we hit these times, but love. Fear desires to creep in at these opportunities to reinforce the optical illusion of distance between 'us and them', but 'Perfect love expels all fear'[3]. Love is the antidote that shows me that my actions could make a real difference to what is happening before my eyes.

After some telephone-guided checks and the consent of the midwife, I look at Steph and give her the word she's been longing to hear, 'push'. To avoid describing all the things you can watch on a good TV documentary, let's just say that within a matter of seconds (literally) he was there, cradled in his mother's arms, our son Eaden. The time was 4:40am. Two minutes later the emergency paramedic was there, another two minutes passed and the stand-by ambulance arrived, with the midwife following at quarter to five.

To this day I am still genuinely saddened that I didn't get to cut the cord.

I don't tell this story to talk about home births or to reinforce the legendary abilities of a good curry (though both would firmly get our recommendations). I tell this story to start our conversation about service. We have already talked about love being expressed through obedience, but it is worth noting that the nature of *service* stands in stark contrast to our understanding of *obedience – obedience* hears and follows, whereas *service* sees and acts.

Love expressed through service perceives need and moves closer with the purpose of bringing change. To begin to serve we must first work to remove the distance between us.

NEIGHBOUR

It's a word that speaks of proximity, closeness and care. You don't hear the word *neighbour* and think about a journey of a thousand miles. But when a man asks Jesus the question, 'Who is my neighbour?', I get the sense that he's not trying to calculate who he needs to get close to, but is seeking clarification (maybe even permission) on who he can keep at a distance. Who does he need / not need to express love to?

The account takes place in Luke 10:25-37. It's a famous passage of scripture; even if you don't know where it is, or have never actually read it, or even opened a bible, the story it contains is one that I am sure you have heard – 'The Good Samaritan'.

The origin of the tale is a question, raised by a man asking Jesus how he can receive eternal life. The form of the man's question is simply, 'How do I get from here to there?', 'How do I get from A to B?' – in a nutshell it is a question about his own personal progression, about his journey. It's a question that only sees self and a distance to be travelled. This might seem a selfish question to ask, but haven't we all asked this at some point? Maybe we don't ask about eternal life, we might even question its existence, but we have all asked questions about our own personal progression; 'What results do I need to achieve in my exams?', 'What do I need to do to get a promotion?', 'Are we there yet?', 'Can you tell me where I can find the milk?' There is nothing immoral with questions of this nature – you could even say that they are the right questions to ask if we are meant to be people who think about the future. Regardless of the question's content, the bottom line is that we are all keenly interested in our own destination; a distance that once traversed will hopefully result in a better and more satisfied version of our current selves.

Jesus' answer to the 'A to B' question is to quote two verses from the Old Testament:

> *'"Love the Lord your God with all your heart, all*
> *your soul, all your strength and all your mind".*
> *And "Love your Neighbour as Yourself"* [4]

It is here that the man raises his second query, the question I indicated at the beginning of this section: *'Who is my neighbour?'* His first question was a legitimate question to ask, but it is this question that reveals something of the heart of the man. The passage tells us that the man asks this question to 'justify his actions' (the New King James Version says to 'justify himself') – this is a man who knows that there are already some relationships that exist in his life where distance has been removed, and others where distance has been cultivated. It would be easy to judge the man, but he's just asking questions that I'm sure we all have asked, giving voice to things we maybe have never verbalised. His question certainly finds its echo from within me; I am an expert at cultivating space – am I the only person who is?

It's worth saying at this point, that the word for *neighbour* that is used in Luke 10 is the Greek word *plēsion* – literally meaning 'near'. This is not a neighbour in the sense of a shared nationality (*geitōn*), or the person we dwell next to (*perioikos*). So the *who* of *neighbour* being discussed here isn't a conversation about the identity of others, loaded with preconceived ideas about ethnicity or sharing the same neighbourhood – it is purely a measure of the physical distance between people and not a value statement about the people involved[5]. We could say that to *'love your neighbour'* is to *'Love the One You're With'* (to quote Luther Vandross[6]), regardless of class, colour, age, gender, creed or morals.

So I totally get the man's response to this statement; my 21st century echo to this man's 1st century question would be: 'Love all people! Surely you can't mean *all* people? Surely there are people I don't have to *love*? Can I not stop at just liking some people?'

My world is full of people, networks of individuals who fall into all sorts of categories: friends, family, close family, neighbours (in the shared street context), strangers, colleagues, associates, peers, service providers, commuters, fellow social networkers, enemies... It isn't just 'people I know' and 'people I don't know' – there are many integrated layers in between. *My world* is full of varying degrees of distance. But Jesus takes all these divisions and boxes them altogether and says 'neighbour' – love them all! It's important to see here that Jesus is not saying we should love all people the same, Jesus is not saying love your enemy like you love your kids – He is saying love them all like you love yourself.

This call to love our neighbour is not a call to just love the people who we share a resemblance with, but *all* who we move in close distance to. It is not just a call to love those who we share common interests with, but to *all* who we share space and time with. Apparently, my progress through my own 'A-B' process is not really about my actual progress, but really about the connection I develop with others also in process.

NAKED

Jesus responds to our question by telling a story, and so a conversation that was initiated by a man concerned with his own distance to travel has now evolved into a story about a man – a Jewish man, a *geitōn* and *perioikos* – who was also on a journey. However, this man, while travelling, is violently assaulted, robbed, stripped and left for dead at the side of the road – left in a state in which he'll never be able to reach the destination he set out for.

Left stripped and half dead

Naked   Speechless   Expressionless

Take a moment to consider that scene.

Walking past, what would you have seen?

What we wear, how we speak and *how we move* have all become useful terms for us to describe difference; but this man has been stripped of all that would prevent a passer-by describing him in terms that wouldn't also apply to themselves. All they would see is skin, and in his part of the world, at that time in history, would this have been enough to place him in another social bracket from anyone else who would happen to take this road? Maybe if he was front down and had shoulder length hair it might even be impossible to determine his gender or age? I admit that this is possibly pushing the text too much, but see this: he is a person without a label. *We* know he is Jewish because Jesus tells us, but for the other characters who have yet to enter this story, he is just flesh like them; a human being – a human being in need. With the exception of the contrast of life and death, this man leaves no differences for the other characters to use as a basis for their decision to draw near or impose distance. No 'Shibboleth/Sibboleth'[7] test will help them to determine how worthy this man is to receive their time and their care – their service. The choice to help would rest with them and only with them, a choice that can only be based on their ability to perceive this fellow human's need.

If I have no problem in loving myself, then loving people who are like me is no great task – it's loving those who are *different* where the challenge is to be found; and difference is a powerful way to impose distance, in the virtual sense, when none exists in the physical realm. But here is the test that Jesus has staged in this story – even when the differences have been removed and shown as inconsequential, even when our similarities have been exposed – can we still express love through service? The line between loving ourselves and loving our neighbour has suddenly become blurred.

The little boy in the movie *The Sixth Sense* had a problem with seeing dead people – I have heard this movie reference used numerous times in ministry to stir the heart of the church to reach those who are not followers of Jesus. Although I don't necessarily disagree with this application, I don't think it goes deep enough for service. Dead is still different. Dead still provides room for 'us and them' distinctions to be drawn and developed.

Maybe what we really need to see is *naked* people? We need to stop seeing the labels that people wear, or have been given, and we just need to start seeing people. Again, I'm an expert at creating difference-orientated space; 21st century living has honed my ability to compartmentalise every detail in life, so I'm also in need of the Spirit's help to sharply hone my ability to not focus on *what* people are, but *who* people are – they are just like me – flesh. They may be in different packaging, from different environments, with different experiences of life leading them to make different choices – but they are still me.

Our acts of service cannot be given or withheld on the basis of the status and the social category that those we move in close proximity to fall into, regardless of whether people are labelled Jew, rich, poor, gay, addict, enemy, transgender, clergyman, celebrity, prostitute, single parent... stripped down, we're all just skin. People in need, people on journeys, people with a destination. The motive to serve is love, a love that flows because we see the *us* in *them*.

Who will see the naked and close the gap?

SEEING IS BELIEVING

Jesus continues telling His parable; a Jewish priest walks past...

> '...but when he saw him lying there, he crossed to the other side of the road and passed him by' (NLT).

Do you feel the sense of distance that is spoken in those words; 'when he *saw* him lying *there*'? 'There' is a word we normally use to describe another location from the one that we presently occupy. For the priest in this story this 'there' was in his direction of travel, just ahead of him, this 'there' was something he would soon encounter – something that carried the potential to become a part of his own journey. However, the priest doesn't even come close, the priest saw him 'there' and chooses to cross over – 'there' never becomes 'here'.

I have to ask, but what could he have really seen from such distance? How much definition and detail of the situation could he have understood to base this decision on? I suspect very little. Whatever he glimpsed was enough to label this need as an obstacle to his own destination. He saw nothing that gave him justification to serve – what he saw wasn't even worthy enough to merit his concern. His choice to create distance here, to alter course, was based on ignorance. I can't help but wonder that when he finally passed by the man, did he look or did he continue to avert his eyes from the detail?

Some scholars try to give reason (not excuse) for this fictitious priest's actions, some based on the direction of his journey – whether he was on his way to Jerusalem, or on his way to Jericho. But Jesus doesn't state the priest's journey in either direction, and neither does Jesus himself place within the story any reason for the crossing over – except that he *saw*.

Ignorance really is bliss. The less I'm aware of, the more likely I am to not serve. Service requires the ability to see, and often to see up close. If I can choose what I allow myself to focus on, I can censor what causes my heart to be moved. 'Selfishness only sees oneself' to quote something I heard a friend say recently. I am just as guilty as the priest in this story – it's demonstrated through my use of the television remote and in the time difference between the transitions of certain pages within magazines and newspapers. If I am totally honest, when the post arrives full of 'junk mail', it is the leaflets marked 'sale', not the ones printed with images of the victims of inhumanity and disease that appeal to me. My selfishness leads me to regulate what I label as junk; what is an opportunity and what is an obstacle. My eyes want to screen everything – but could censorship in this way possibly be immoral? *Ignorance*, like *difference*, is another way to reinforce the space between us and them.

However, there are those moments when my peripheral space is intruded on, leaving my heart exposed to bliss-rupturing reality:

I remember going to watch the film *Saving Private Ryan*; in the opening scenes the brutality of World War II battle really hit me as the allied troops landed on the beaches of Normandy. I had seen war films prior to this, both non-fiction and fiction, but in this film people lost limbs, blood flowed without a care for my preferences, lives ended, friends were lost, field paramedics fought losing battles to save the injured, terror and fear screamed for my attention. This was not action entertainment; this wasn't cars crashing into helicopters or giant robots trashing whole city blocks – it's easier to view those sorts of movies and to hold *here* and *there* as totally separate concepts. But from the first ten minutes alone, this film had clearly stated its message – here's the reality of warfare. I couldn't take my eyes off the film. I wanted to, but in a dark cinema, where the only source of light is the screen itself, I had no other distractions to focus on. To avert my eyes was not an option and even if I closed my eyes, my ears would still remain wide open. It was a truly shocking experience, but one that I am thankful for.

Not long ago I attended a church conference; one of the seminars was headed by a young man named Ben Cooley, the co-founder of a charity called *Hope for Justice*[8]. During his keynote speech, which took place before the morning break, he showed a video documenting the physical and emotional torment experienced by a young woman who had been the victim of human trafficking. It was brutal. I physically couldn't move when the morning break came, I sat there weeping, my heart broken and my innocence rightly violated by the story I had just seen. Again, like war, I had known about human trafficking for a while, I *saw* it *there* – but this video brought its details firmly into focus.

I could recount further examples of when my mind's eye has been forcefully moved on to the predicaments of others – by books, by conversations, by walks through local streets and prayer meetings and visits to foreign countries. But eventually, time has its way and the distance is recreated. I close the book, I leave the cinema, the conversation ends and in the passing days, unless I allow my mind to reminisce, my ignorance is restored to its own self-inclined equilibrium. My sight fixes itself once again on my own destination. *I begin to fill the screen.*

I wonder how long it was in his journey down the road before the priest forgot the plight that he had just witnessed.

I suspect that there are many of us who have played the part of the priest, our own sense of destination greatly overshadowing that of others – but God asks of us to see.

> *'Share each other's burdens, and in this way obey the law of Christ. If you think you are too important to help someone, you are only fooling yourself. You are not that important.'*[9]

To serve requires us to see reality, and to keep that reality centred within our vision. Until we do, the naked, downtrodden and robbed of this world will remain lining the roads of life.

UNTOUCHABLE

The body remains beside the road, but the story gives us another chance of rescue. A temple worker, a Levite, is also taking the same road. The priest, a man of contemplation, failed to contemplate, but the Levite – he's a man of action, a servant by reputation, a doer. Jesus tells us that, unlike the priest, this man closes the distance and 'walked over and looked at him lying there'.

Time passes here as the Levite assesses the situation; he's studying the details, evaluating the severity of the wounded man's condition, but eventually '... he also passed by on the other side'. The Levite sees the reality, but chooses not to serve, leaving reality unchanged.

Again, Jesus doesn't give us the reasons for this action-man's decision to do nothing. Maybe it is a good thing that Jesus doesn't; if he had, would that one reason have been elevated by ourselves to be the only non-legitimate reason for not aiding someone? Would we then impose into this text some of our own valid reasons for declining assistance?

Biblical scholars give the Levite the same reason for his crossing-over as the priest; they are both concerned about touching a dead body – and I suppose the man does look dead. Leviticus 19:11-22, stipulated that anyone who touched a dead body would be ceremonially unclean – this rule would have been at the forefront of both the priest's and the Levite's minds. But this 'uncleanness' wasn't a permanent thing – the rules given in the Old Testament are not saying, 'Don't touch dead people – ever!' In essence they simply say, 'You will, you should, but after you do, be cleansed'. Either the men misunderstood this (which I doubt), or they were each conscious of the delay that would be caused to their own journeys if they did touch this corpse – a seven day delay to their agendas. Their focus on 'self' made them both unwilling to risk touch.

Credit has to be given to the temple worker; at least he looked prior to making his decision. Perhaps the intensity of his looking was to try and determine if the man was dead or alive, indicating that he was willing to help – as long as the cost to himself was not detrimental? But his actions, although based on reflection, are identical to those of his predecessor. There is no ignorance in this temple worker's choice to move on, but that doesn't mean that he walked away with the truth of the situation. After all, he classifies a living man as a dead man, 'some hope' as 'beyond hope'.

I'm a dad, so from experience I can tell you that it's not always easy to tell life from death. When both our boys did their time in the *Moses basket* beside our bed, Steph would laugh at me as I would sit there for minutes on end trying to work out if our sons were breathing or not. They were both silent snoozers – in fact I slept better when they snored. Trying to spot an infant's chest rise and fall under layers made up of baby grows, blankets and quilts is like trying to catch grass growing. Eventually, the only way for me to gain any peace of mind, would be to lay my hand upon their chest, to connect, by allowing their movement to become my movement.

It's not always easy to distinguish life from death by just looking, so I wonder how close this temple-worker got. Did he bend down? Did he put an ear to the man's mouth? How close would he allow himself to get? How close was too close? I have this surreal picture forming in my mind of him trying to hover over the man, placing his body in awkward positions in his attempt to discover truth without touching, kind of like some surreal ancient game of *Twister*. However he carried out his experiment, his only method of investigation was to look – no mention is made to him trying to talk to the man or even poke him with a stick! He wouldn't even risk delay in the pursuit of truth.

As mentioned with the birth story earlier, looking isn't enough to make us aware of the situations of others; it is only when all our senses are involved in the discovery of truth that we fully become aware of reality. For example, when the bible encourages us to experience God, it isn't just some intellectual gathering of more information; the bible encourages us to discover Him with the whole of our being – the scriptures are filled with exhortations to hear, see, taste, touch and know. To experience reality is a multi-sensory event.

Therefore, service requires connection. Real connection is allowing the movements of others to find symmetry in our own movements. Nowhere is this more evident than when people engage in mission. You can have endless amounts of visiting speakers coming and sharing their experiences from the mission field, slide show presentations, glossy brochures and video documentaries, but nothing produces that symmetry of movement within people like when they actually go and dwell with others; sharing their life experiences, breathing their air, walking their streets, doing life together. How can we 'share each other's burdens' if we all walk at different tempos?

John's gospel tells us that God, the Word, was so filled with love for us that 'the Word became human'[10] – even in His own mission to serve humanity, Jesus would have been powerless if He had just looked down on us from up on high. God does not play *twister* with Humanity.

The temple-worker might have closed the physical distance between himself and the body, but his subconscious had already reinforced the space by deciding that this man was *untouchable*. He had already decided that this man's rhythm was not going to affect his own.

Was his looking really about seeking clarification or about seeking confirmation, peace of mind, for his already-made decision to not act? At least then he could continue on his way without any sense of guilt.

Could it be that occasionally we avoid serving because we feel our actions cannot make a difference – it is already too late; and that sometimes we seek information not to awaken ourselves to the needs that exist, but to validate our reasons for not engaging? Maybe sometimes we even feel that to inquire is to serve. Looking, we feel, is enough of a gesture of love?

It's easy to cross-over; when life is focused on me it is less messy, it's a cleaner, nicer and smoother-going road over on the other side. However, the minute life starts to be about others, things get complicated, resources get stretched and time becomes tighter, our own pace becomes slower – maybe even changing the course of our own destination. But the *untouchable* attitude will leave people without help to reach their own journey's end. It's simpler to keep things *untouchable*; after all, the moment contact is made we become infected.

It seems that the only sure way of making me see the issues that exist are the times when 'need' decides to ambush me on my own journey through life, not only causing me to notice the reality and details, but to be touched by them. Sometimes the only time I really begin to see, to have empathy, is when *there* becomes *here* – a family member is taken by cancer and I then begin to support a cancer research charity; redundancy takes place and I suddenly become aware of the real financial struggles other friends have to travel through and the assistance they need; a child is diagnosed as not being neurotypical and our hearts are opened to the support and friendship families require; you have a mental breakdown and suddenly you realise how fragile we all are and how easy it is to overload people's lives with demands and burdens.

LOVE IN THE MOST UNLIKELY OF PLACES

The story's looking hopeless at this point; I imagine the crowd listening to Jesus were thinking the same as we are: 'How could anyone abandon such a man? How could anyone walk past? Will no one help?' The heroes they would have expected to be a source of help to the beaten traveller have already passed by – the priest and the Levite; those who appear to excel in their devotion to God, those who seem to flourish in their ability to achieve the requirement of the first and greatest commandment, but they are both shown to struggle in the second. Maybe their visible struggle with the second commandment really speaks of their invisible struggle with the first?

It's important for us to realise that when Jesus uses a priest and a Levite, He isn't having a poke at all religious people; these men represent all men. It isn't just the religious and the ritualised among humanity who struggle with apathy and a lack of empathy. We are all committed to becoming better versions of ourselves, but if this isn't guided then we all face the possibility of *me* becoming our only focus.

The essence of service is about taking a vested interest in the journeys of those who also travel life's road. From the bandits, to the priest, to the Levite – everyone who has come across this man so far has had no other journey in mind except their own. What's next?

Jesus introduces His final character – a Samaritan. If this were a pantomime production, this would be the point when the kids in the audience would be booing and hissing and shouting, 'He's behind you'. Any good bible commentary will tell you of the disdain that the Jews and the Samaritans held towards each other. From the Jewish perspective in Jesus' audience, this was a man who visibly struggled with the practice of loving God with all his strength, mind, heart and soul – if he so clearly fails in the first how would he ever succeed in loving his neighbour, let alone his enemy?

But it is this third man that Jesus makes the hero; the man who is neither *perioikos* nor *geitōn* shows us what it is to be *plēsion*.

The stage is the same as it was for the previous two travellers; the Samaritan is greeted with the same nakedness that met both the priest and the Levite. But the catalyst that causes the difference in reaction this time around is not environmental, it isn't even because the man is a Samaritan – it is simply the insertion of a few little words: 'he felt deep pity*' (*splanchnizomai* – it's that movement of the innards again, Love). This is something that every human is capable of feeling. Love made the difference.

Love saw life where others saw death.

Love caused empathy where others had decided merely to evaluate.

Love considered.

Love moved closer.

Love touched.

Love served.

Love, without the need of some external cry, chooses to stop and make a difference to this man's course.

Love was the difference between a Samaritan, a Priest and a Levite.

LOVING GOD

Jesus tells another story with a similar heart to this one in Matthew's gospel 25:31-46 – it's a story about dividing people from each other like dividing sheep from goats. The people in question are those who call Him 'Lord', again people who feel they have mastered this first commandment. But a division is being made all the same – those who really served Him, from those who didn't.

The King in this parable uses their acts of service towards him as the benchmark for his choices, but as the King explains, their acts of service were not towards him, but towards the least of his brothers and sisters. Those acts involved the provision of food and water, clothing, medicine and aid, shelter and companionship, towards their fellow man.

The practicality of these things really strikes me; the simplicity of them to fulfil really humbles me. Serving people is not something that most of us in the western world lack the resources to do – but again the problem lies with our *seeing* and our *connecting*.

We read that both groups are shocked and surprised by the King's decision, both groups respond with the same question:

> '"When did we ever see you hungry and feed you? Or thirsty and give you something to drink? Or a stranger and show you hospitality? Or naked and give you clothing? When did we ever see you sick or in prison, and visit you?" ' [11]

For those labelled 'sheep', as they journeyed through life, they saw need and practised the art of being *plēsion*. They simply saw others, and served. They didn't even think of it as serving God. But it was.

The 'goats'? They also saw, but they failed to connect. Maybe they waited for some instruction, some command, some external call they could practise obedience to? Seeing wasn't enough for them, they needed to be asked. They too, didn't even think of it as serving God, but it was!

To serve Jesus it seems, according to these parables, is to serve humanity, to serve each other. After all, what needs does God have?[12]

Please understand me here; I am not having a conversation about how to experience salvation. The truth is we have all failed in the practice of both loving God and loving people – these parables just underscore our grades, we are *all* in need of the grace of God. No amount of serving people, no amount of works will help us *earn* eternal life – that sort of thinking just pops us back into the mechanical vending machine view of life. We must remember that it took God coming and serving humanity through the pouring out His life, for the gift of salvation to be made available.

What I am talking about however, is that so often I ask myself, we ask ourselves, 'How can I serve God?' We get so tied up in waiting for commands and prompts and calls that we become immobile; we become so focused on our own spiritual journey that we have made our cause an assault course and not a relationship with our creator. Hopefully this will be a releasing thought – 'What can I do to serve God?' The answer is all around us. Look at the people you share time and space with and you'll see God's response. Maybe the progress of our journey isn't measured by the distance we travel, but by the relationships we form – the distance between us?

Love God, Love People. We are all capable of this, it doesn't take superpowers.

~~MORE THAN~~ HUMAN

I find it interesting that we human beings even have this amazing capacity to want the best, or simply what is right, for someone other than ourselves. Within our world there are people who are examples of this kind of love in motion every day; making sacrifices, spending money, using their talents and their time – all for the benefit of *other*. Why would people behave like this? Why should people spend their energy, their resources, and their days on the needs of somebody else? This doesn't sound like a survival of the fittest mentality, or something that would arise out of some mutation of our genes. Eminent geneticist Francis Collins presents the puzzle like this, *'Agape, or selfless altruism, presents a major challenge for the evolutionist. It is quite frankly a scandal to reductionist reasoning. It cannot be accounted for by the drive of individual selfish genes to perpetuate themselves. Quite the contrary: it may lead humans to make sacrifices that lead to great personal suffering, injury, or death, without any evidence of benefit. And yet, if we carefully examine that inner voice we sometimes call conscience, the motivation to practice this kind of love exists within all of us, despite our frequent efforts to ignore it'.*[13]

Human history is littered with examples of people who poured out their lives in the act of serving humanity, with very little return to themselves; Mother Teresa, William Wilberforce, Oskar Schindler, Jesus, to name just a few. We are inspired by these people. We see their actions as noble and right, and we hold them up as examples of virtue. Not once would we remark that their sacrifices, their acts of service, were nothing more than sentimentalism or a gush of romantic feelings. Something within each of us acknowledges that their actions express something of the pure, untainted nature of love. But despite our acknowledgement of this, if these heroes and their unsung contemporaries walked into our own *Dragon's Den*, they probably wouldn't get our investment. There is something about their lives that, even though inspiring, is also terrifying; it seems to lack a business plan – it doesn't even appear to contain any business sense. Their sales pitch would be empty of words like profit, gain and return, the chart showing their five-year plan would appear to be upside down and their concept of people would not be as potential investors in the latest product, but as the beneficiaries of all they have and hold. Service is scary, we all understand that it means letting go of something we have, maybe even everything. True selfless altruism is something we admire, but few aspire to.

Here is the difficulty I have, the difficulty that seems to crop up in conversation when talking about serving others; I admire these people so much (and I should) that I have begun to use them to define my own unsuitability and inferiority. I have made their acts of service so great, that the idea of service has become something that only takes place if it is *great* and done by *great* and extraordinary people.

Even the 'Good Samaritan' has become a hero instead of the traveller that Jesus describes him as. Jesus never once lifts the man above his own cultural identity; he could be anyone – even our enemy. Jesus tells us that the man was a Samaritan, but it was us that gave him the label 'good', as if to separate him from the norm. Have I, in honouring the deeds and acts of others, created for myself an excuse to once again impose distance between myself and the needs of the world around me? After all, I'm not as great a servant as they are/were, can I really make a difference?

It would be different if I had superpowers, then I could do something really significant. If I was more than just a human maybe then I could really bring change. If had super strength, invincibility, super-cool gadgets or could web-sling, then I would have the powers that the world needs (admittedly, the last one was more about me). But it doesn't take special abilities to provide food and clothing, even the abilities listed in 1 Corinthians 12 that the Holy Spirit gives can't provide these! It requires love.

I am conscious that in writing a chapter about service that our minds can automatically gravitate to the *great deeds* done by those *great people*, and when that happens there is always the temptation to disregard the acts we already do, and the people we already serve. We can allow the shadow cast by these monuments to instil within us a feeling that our works just don't measure up, that our acts aren't enough to be called significant.

I am convinced that service can be simple and powerfully significant, especially when love is involved. When love becomes the motive to serve, it stops being defined on a scale between *great* and *simple*; it becomes *essential*. Only when love is absent from our acts do we feel the need to measure our deeds and determine if they are worthy of merit. Love doesn't measure the task. Love places its value in the one it serves. Surely a heart that loves people will always seek to serve the people it loves?

Take parents, for example. Our children have the best butlers, cleaners, manicurists, personal shoppers, dressers, chefs, chauffeurs, life coaches, counsellors, huggers, groupies, entertainers and event organisers that money just can't afford – and we do it all for nothing. Out of a deep desire to want the best for our children, we serve.

No parent serves their children out of a need for gratitude and appreciation. Though it may have been naively wanted at the start, I would have been heartbroken if my son's first words were 'Thank-you' and not 'Dada'! In fact, it can take years before our children really begin to see all that we have done for them and what it cost for us to do it. As a thirty-something father of two, only now have I started to gain a glimpse of the sacrifices of my own mother and father.

No parent hopes for some eventual return from their investment either, although I do hope my children will honour their mum and dad when they're older. It's purely that we love them; we want them to be all that they are able to become – the return we seek isn't monetary or time, but them. We long for them to reach their destination. We have chosen to invest our journey into theirs.

So when I talk about service I'm really thinking about the little stuff, the things we all could do. Things that don't require major geographical changes to our lifestyle, but often only require a relocation of our heart. If service closes up the space between us, then that can mean the laying down of our life, but it can also mean just simply picking up a towel.

Jesus is always our reference point. When I think about the two greatest acts of His servanthood, the washing of the disciples' feet and His dying on the cross, I realise that He performed both of these acts without clinging to His rights as God. He didn't skip the effort and cost required in either of these moments by using His super, more than human, rights or powers. He became human[14]. His love for humanity moved Him to take the position of a servant, becoming nothing, yet both of these acts continue to affect, transform and restore the journeys of millions.

I am convinced that sometimes, God's greatest miracles take place out of the fullness of the human capacity to serve.

'Do not withhold good from those who deserve it when it's in your power to help them' – Proverbs 3:27 (NLT)

'If we love our brothers and sisters, it proves that we have passed from death to eternal life. But a person who has no love is still dead... let us stop just saying we love each other; let us really show it by our actions' – 1 John 3:14 & 18

EXPRESSED THROUGH **WORSHIP**

'To have found God and still to pursue
Him is the soul's paradox of love'
A.W.Tozer[1]

NOISE

I've always had a passion for music. I can't help it really, I grew up in a home where songs were sown into the fabric of daily life.

Both my parents were born in the nineteen forties, and my five brothers and I were born between the mid-seventies and early eighties; as a consequence our house buzzed with a catalogue of sixty plus years of music: *Elvis, Erasure, W.A.S.P, Doris Day, U2, Simon & Garfunkel, ABBA, Bon Jovi, Nat King Cole, Tchaikovsky, The Carpenters, Nirvana, Don McLean, The Beatles, Alanis Morissette* and even *Patsy Cline.*

Of course the inevitable clashes occurred over who was playing music and who was just making noise, and yes, this usually took place between brothers. We rarely agreed, and sometimes that disagreement would turn nasty! Two of my brothers often got into full on fist fights just because of their difference in opinion about *Bobbie Brown* – their bedroom door bearing most of the scars. But now, although we've grown up (physically speaking) and our tastes have diverged even more, we've found common ground with our parents' songs – none of us will complain if *Crazy*, sung by *Patsy Cline,* comes on the radio. It resonates with us, not because we're all *'crazy for feeling so blue'*, but because the melody evokes memory – a memory of our childhood together, collective memories of our exploits, our achievements, our failures – *our* growing up. When our parents' songs play, those songs stop being *sensed* and start being *shared*. As they play, our individual identities, memories and feelings start to replay into something more corporate. *We* hear, and the past, present and future suddenly meet in one place.

Music somehow carries this potential for synergy.

This is why every human culture and sub-culture has its own particular style of music, why every generation has its 'tunes', and why each friendship has its songs; because there exists within each music genre an exhaustive catalogue of lyrics and melodies that somehow embody and generate the whole spectrum of human emotion and experience. And in our attempts to explore our self – as we move towards the rhythms and refrains that we feel provide an echo to our innermost identity – we nearly always find ourselves uncovering and rediscovering other people along the way as well.

Sound seems to provide a context for connections to take place.

I can't have been the only one to experience something like this, but, have you ever found yourself in a car, or at home, or in a shop... when suddenly a song comes on the radio that you haven't heard for over a decade? If someone had asked you to write the lyrics of that song down prior to hearing it, you would have struggled, but with the music playing you find the words almost naturally flowing out from your lips. Whatever the tempo, it seems to help shake the dust and cobwebs off the past. But it's not only the words that come flooding back – anchored to those words are our stories, some that we delight in, others we want to forget.

I hear Bon Jovi's *You give love a bad name*, and in my mind I'm taken back to being seven, playing on the field near my childhood home and revelling in the freedom of just being a kid. When I hear *Champagne Supernova* by *Oasis*, I remember a teenage kiss (it's a long song!). When we sing Hillsong's *My Jesus, My Saviour* in our gatherings, I can't help but think back to that little church service when I finally let the wall down to Jesus. I hear *Cavatina*, and I'm once again at my father's funeral, witnessing the heartbreak etched on my brothers' faces. And when *Patsy Cline* sings *Crazy*, well, I feel the warmth of my mum once again – it's almost as if I can hear her voice singing along too.

They're never just songs are they? They're soundtracks to the scenes of our lives.

And it's not only songs that do this, the same thing happens with all the other sounds too, the everyday sounds, like the flow of traffic, the buzz of a lawnmower, or the sound of a ticking clock against the silence of night-time. And neither is it just with the things we hear – our memories seem to leak out of odours, and tastes, and colours, and textures. Everyday things stop being *just* everyday things, they become altars of sorts, reminding us of something else, speaking of something that they aren't.

It's never just noise, never just a bit of parkland, never just the smell of freshly-baked bread, never just a cross... never just a human.

SYMBOLS

To a great extent our society depends on symbols so much that we probably take them for granted, but they're everywhere, our modern world is swamped with them. They surround us in varying camouflaged blends of shapes, colours and sounds: road signs, tattoos, logos, ringtones... a pre-schooler's crayoned picture of his home, the angle of Steph's eyebrows when I've said something I shouldn't have, even the singular isolated spot that occurs at the end of this sentence. All these symbols tell us something.

Even the words contained in this book are symbolic, recognised forms that speak of something they don't physically resemble – take *wristwatch* for example; the word itself doesn't look anything like the timekeeping device that's worn at the end of a limb. But those who recognise and understand the certain arrangement of lines that is *wristwatch* will know what it's referring too. This is how symbolism works – the symbol bears an image, but not necessarily its own. And when the use of symbols is used to full effect, communication of an image is no longer limited by our proximity to each other – with the right symbol I don't have to be with you to show you something, I can communicate to you without being hindered by the restrictions of time and space.

The trick is trying to find the right symbol, one that every other human can understand, one that applies whatever context they find themselves in.

The bible is full of symbolism, from rainbows and vineyards to arranged piles of stone (altars), BBQs of manure (don't ask – actually, do ask!) and bread and wine. These symbols speak of God's interactions within the cosmos, or people's understandings of them, but they don't necessarily speak of God. What I mean by that is this, that when God talked with Noah about the rainbow, He didn't say 'When you look at that rainbow Noah, that's Me, in glorious "Technicolor"' – the symbol of the rainbow simply functions as a reminder of a promise God made[2], its colour and pattern evokes memory. Even the Temple, probably one of the most important icons of the Old and New Testaments isn't an image of God.

Actually, the infamous Ten Commandments strictly forbid making an image of God. Which can seem a bit OTT. What is God saying here? Is He forbidding artistic licence? Does He have a problem with marketing and logos? Is He kind of saying, 'No pictures please' like they do at concerts? Maybe God knows that these things can escalate – first you start with a statue and then eventually, somewhere down the line, someone is going to try and improve it by covering it with lots of tiny seashells! Or, and seriously now, could it actually be that God is saying that He doesn't need one, He already has one – He has already called and crafted for Himself a symbol to bear His image?

In the first chapter of Genesis we are told that people were made in the image of God –

'So God created people in his own image; God patterned them after himself; male and female he created them'[3]

There have been countless discussions over the years as to what this means; does God have literal arms, and legs, and even hair follicles in some sort of divine nostrils? Is it simply talking about our personalities and characteristics – that we can think, create, laugh, love? I'm not sure I'm clever enough to take on these kinds of questions. But in keeping with our train of thought so far, what if humanity is itself a symbol, or at least should be functioning as one, a symbol that should be speaking of something larger and outside itself? What if *we* are meant to be the taste, sound and odour of God via our interactions with each other, our work, our play, in the midst of our creativity and even in our rest?[4] Can humanity, through its care of each other, and through its care of the world it lives in, show us God?

This is one of the reasons that I felt writing this book was important. We live in a world that struggles to believe in the existence of the divine. Using various methods of investigation, we go searching under rocks, we probe outer space, and even peek into the midst of cellular life and the atomic world, trying to get a glimpse of the potential of some maker. It's a shame that we have to go so far to try and see the image of the divine. Of course, depending on the thinking of the observer, some will declare they have found traces of God, while others do not – their perspectives are never that objective. Regardless of how close we look, our subjective viewpoint has been formed by the larger image we see clearly every day – humanity. Some see its suffering, the wars, the famines...most of which are self-propagated or self-sustained through greed, and conclude that there can't be a God. What we do speaks of God.

Before I'm stoned for heresy here – I am not saying that I'm God, or that you're God, or that *we* are God. Remember the example; the word wristwatch isn't a watch – but its form testifies of it. If that doesn't make any sense, then maybe the Apostle Paul's picture of us being like mirrors to reflect God's glory hopefully will[5].

I'm saying all this because when we talk about worship, often the conversation gets hung up on choruses and hymns and tempo, or noise versus silence, or the use of tambourines, but I'm not talking about that. If worship is only about musical ability, then what about the people who don't have any of that ability, what about those who don't like singing, and what about people like me who have a phobia of tambourines, can they be worshippers? I'm all for our singing together; as I said at the start of this chapter, song is powerful in bringing us together and expressing our experiences, but worship is not limited to music – worship is about the transmission of our lives. It's about who/what our lives speak of. It's not a measure of how engaged we are with singing, but of how we engage in life.

What's love got to do with it? (Yep, that's a song title, sorry)

Love expressed through worship is not about serenading God, so don't panic if that's what you thought when you first saw the chapter heading! Actually, it's much scarier than that. To express love through worship is to care about the other's image and the transmission of that image. To honour someone is to think about what we say about them, how we present them to others, and to even consider what we do in their name[6].

MORE THAN WORDS

I'm told that the average man speaks approximately seven thousand words a day, while the average woman exceeds that by a further thirteen thousand – I don't know how true these statistics are, or whether the difference really is simply down to a particular protein (Foxp2). I'm also doubtful as to whether this difference exists at all, especially after recently reading Cordelia Fine's *Delusions of Gender*. Either way, that's a lot of words. As a quick comparison, the word count in each chapter of this book is approximately the same as an average man's daily quota (whatever an 'average' man is?).

But, just in case you misunderstood the idiom I used about worship being what our lives speak of, I'm not talking just about our words.

Our eldest son is obsessed with *Lego*. I mean, he's nuts about it – every studded cuboid of it. The very blocks that my bare feet fear to embrace, he seeks and rejoices in. His perfect day would consist of sitting in a room full of *Lego* sets, all needing to be constructed, and then dismantled, and then rebuilt again. He memorises set numbers. He knows how many pieces his most coveted sets contain. He knows facts, and set release dates, and... well, anything else he can discover. "When I'm grown up, I'm going to leave home and move to Denmark and work for *Lego*" is what he fondly reminds us, his loving and doting parents, nearly every day. I once asked him what he loves more, 'Mummy and Daddy' *or* '*Lego*'; his answer was both! And that answer only came after a very long, reflective pause.

Our youngest son (the one Steph and I have nicknamed 'Magpie') loves junk. Well, I consider it junk, but to him it's treasure. Random stuff that the average person (there's that word average again) wouldn't give any value to what-so-ever. But to him, it's worth keeping, cherishing and protecting. Our youngest goes nowhere without the backpack that acts as his portable cache of odds and ends – he refuses, far too often, to leave this stuff behind. He wants a gerbil for his birthday, but I'm afraid it will end up in the backpack, squeezed between sweets that have had five weeks to fester, a cuddly toy and scraps of tinfoil.

For both of them, their intentions, their actions, the investment of their time, energy and imagination, their loyalty – they all speak of something *other*, using a language that is far larger than syllables. But we understand this about love – it's more than words. The bottom line is that love doesn't speak solely of itself – not unless it's narcissistic.

However, to worship is deeper than this. To worship something is to hold it in a place of glory. I've heard it said many times, that the thing we worship becomes the centre of our lives. The analogy often used is similar to our solar system – that we hold *a* thing central in our lives, like our Sun, which we then revolve around. But I want to change that picture, because, like our own solar system we actually have more than one focal point that we orbit[7], and I personally feel that that's fine.

It's ok to love your family. It's ok to love playing golf – if that's what you enjoy. It's ok to read, and to study, and to work. It's ok to have your favourite TV shows and 'boy bands'. Dare I say it, to some extent it's even ok to love your tech and gadgets so much that you're prepared to queue outside a store all night (although, personally I do feel this a tad materialistic). The thing is, we carry the potential to hold many things central to our lives – and that's fine. I don't believe this makes us worshippers of them. And often, I have seen followers of Christ feel guilty, or be made to feel guilty, just because they enjoy something other than God. Hey, that's ok!

So to change the metaphor, what you worship is not what you orbit in your own little solar system of life – what we worship becomes our universe. What we choose to love above all others provides the context, the environment, the laws, the energy and the matter that ultimately defines the nature of our movement about the things we orbit.

Love expressed through worship is to allow that one love, that one chief commitment of our will, to permeate and flavour all our other loves. hat's why we can love many things, but you can only really worship one thing, at any one time. What we love taints the expression of that love. Whatever we choose to worship controls the narrative of our story; it tells us who the story is about.

In the bible, worship is reserved only for God. The same set of commandments that call us not to make images of God, begin with the appeal that we shouldn't worship any other gods, except The God. Again, for some of us, this may seem a bit extreme, but when we couple this with the forbidding of idol-making, it makes some logical sense – the story's about God, and He has called us, humanity, to play His part in the scenes that unfold within creation.

The problem is that we often just want to speak of ourselves, and maybe push the responsibility of looking like God onto a particular someone/something else. This is why God's prohibition to the Hebrew people of making idols makes sense. Especially when we remember that the people who originally heard this command had been slaves in a nation where their deities were always represented by some fancy piece of carving, where some other symbol represented their creator/s. But God doesn't want stonework, He wants flesh, He wants you[8]. Our lives are called to be adjectives of God.

Maybe we don't want the responsibility because we feel we may fail, or that we aren't 'good enough' for the role[9] and so we push God's image on to something else, maybe those who we feel are more divinely called to speak of Him, like pastors and priests. Maybe we want to push the responsibility onto a particular style of worship, or a certain movement of water, or a religious denomination, or a special time of year, or a sunset, or a car bumper sticker, or even a building. Some are contented enough to even let their money make the declaration instead of their lifestyles.

WHOSE IMAGE?

So Jesus is sitting in the midst of an audience within the Temple courts, holding up a Roman coin for all to see, while He asks the question, 'Whose picture and title are stamped on it?'[10]. The coin in question was a denarius, and on it was the image of a face, and an inscription declaring who the face belonged to. In this case, the picture is that of Emperor Tiberius Caesar, and the words inscribed with it declared Tiberius as being divine.

This wasn't *just* a coin.

Coins were the biggest form of media coverage of that day. They still are today, too. If today's businesses were given the opportunity, they would have their slogans and logos stamped all over our currency – they would pay money just to get their faces on it! But prior to the advent of magazines and cable TV, if you wanted to tell the world of your power, if you wanted people to know of your empire, if you wanted to talk about you – then the coin was one of the best transmitters around. And, if you wanted to replace a current regime, then you also looked to replace its currency.

Money moves more fluidly than structures such as palaces, monuments and temples, which take a lot of time and resources to build. Money's a lot simpler to translate into different cultures than rules and edicts; people are far more accepting of cash than laws. People can carry it around with them and trade with it wherever they travel. Unlike the way that today's currency exchanges work, back then silver was still silver, regardless of what was printed on it. Coins are mobile technology, so to speak. To use/carry this form of propaganda was to be in support of its campaign, that's why it bore Caesar's icon (and that's why nearly a century after this scene in the Temple, when the Jewish revolutionary Bar Kokhba led a revolt against the Emperor Hadrian, he also made sure he had new coins minted bearing the image of the Temple). Money does talk, symbolically speaking.

This denarius was a symbol of Roman authority; to use this coin was seen by some as an act of homage to the Emperor. To certain Jews, even carrying a coin like this was blasphemous; a clear break of the first and second commandments – and it's Jesus who's holding this symbol up in *the* Temple at Jerusalem!

Except, this coin doesn't belong to Jesus. He's holding it because He's asked to borrow it. And He's only asked to borrow it because He needs it to answer the question that He's just been asked regarding the payment of taxes to Rome. But the question He's been asked isn't just about taxes, it's much bigger than that – the question is symbolic too, symbolic of allegiances, and Messiahship, and Jesus' stance on the Kingdom of God *vs* the Empire of Rome[11]. It's a question designed to test His loyalties – who should be paid tribute, who should receive honour, and how should that honour be given?

'Show me the coin used to pay the tax', Jesus had said, and I imagine Him saying it in the 'Turn out your pockets' kind of tone that head teachers use, you know, the tone that says they already know what they're going to find in there.

They had come to test Jesus, but it wasn't Jesus who had an image and inscription declaring the divinity of Caesar in His purse.

The Gospel accounts don't tell us that there was a pause after Jesus asked to be shown a coin, but I like to imagine that there was one – an awkward silence, followed by some equally awkward shuffling, accompanied with muffled conversations between themselves. I wonder which of those planning to trick Jesus was the first to produce a denarius in such a tense religious environment, an environment buzzing with people gathering to celebrate and remember their ancestors' liberation from an oppressive regime? It's at this point, with the tables now stunningly turned on His interrogators, that Jesus delivers the famous 'Give to Caesar what belongs to him. But everything that belongs to God must be given to God'. (Again, reading my own imagery in here – I like to imagine Jesus cheekily using his thumb to flick the coin back to its owner while He says this).

You see, there's a nation here that is desperate to see God honoured in their land, and they're divided in how it should be done. For some of them, it's impossible for them to honour God with a corrupted temple, for them God's name can't be glorified while they have to live under the oppression of foreign rulers and while they can only trade using 'dirty' money. They feel that the symbols are all wrong, the pictures aren't right – that none of them speak of God. Some of them are so desperate to take these symbols of Land, Temple and Purity back that they are willing to use violence to try and realign the icons. What they don't realise, or maybe they do, is that fighting for these things and arguing about this stuff, says something about God which isn't true of God (it says 'God's pro stuff and anti people'). How they choose to move will speak of the law behind their movements, more than any coin will.

We don't need to have theologically correct inscriptions printed on our cash, we don't need to wait for perfect religious establishments, and we don't have to live in a culture that is 'godly', before we can start to honour God – just give to God what is His. After all, is the larger narrative of the story about a coin and a temple, or is it about Him?

People – people and their actions, people and their interactions, even people in their inaction are God's chosen media, not stuff, not things, not money.

In some ways we haven't really advanced from this temple scene in the past two thousand years. We're still trying to realign the icons and re-establish the correct inscriptions (for example, it seems that every year I hear the argument about how Christmas/Easter should be celebrated). We're still stuck in the thinking that things should carry the *image* more than we do, and we're even prone to forfeit bearing the image, in order to get it engraved onto something else.

Music, buildings, technology – we fall out over these things, we create barriers and boundaries with them, we use them to define who is really worshipping God. Sadly, sometimes I feel that style has just become the new currency. We even leave churches based on it – which means we break away from one community of relationships to another, simply for the sake of *stuff*. We take what could be used in a sacred way and use it to mark out territory, and then through our boasting of the *stuff* we have, we feel the need to evangelise people to 'our thing' – because, we feel, if you don't look or sound like this, you're not really worshipping. However, in our dividing and in our warring and fighting we dishonour God.

We don't have to have a certain style of music before we can worship. We don't have to have slick presentations or a 'hip' Pastor who always seems to get his delivery right. We don't require the perfect building with a more relevant name across its entrance, or a crowd of over five hundred, or the right programme to volunteer ourselves into – these are all just excuses. We can be worshippers here and now, regardless of the surroundings, the culture and the inscriptions, we just need to give to God what is God's.

I love how Jesus puts it, *'For where two or three gather together because they are mine, I am there among them'*[12] – just people, people being together, and the visible image of the invisible God is made manifest. No *stuff* required.

Now please understand, I'm not a puritan (at least, I don't think I am) – I'm not anti things per se. If you have a great building that you meet in – great! If you have crowds of people – fantastic! If you have a guitarist who hammers out riffs like Metallica's Kirk Hammett – then I am, hand on heart, extremely jealous! But our worship shouldn't be dependent on them, because they don't really provide the true context of our worship.

It's our life together that best communicates what God is like. That's why we need church, again, not institutions and buildings, but community – we cannot reflect/see this image alone. This image needs to be transmitted through the plurality and diversity of life together. I think that's why the Apostle Paul likes to refer to the church as the body of Christ, because it's the synergetic movement of people that God has mobilised to be the vehicle of His expression, a loving expression that speaks of a loving God.

The church of today should long not to be known for its buildings, or its music style or its sleek technologically up-to-date presentations but, to use Brennan Manning's terminology, the church should desire to be known as a *'community of professional lovers'*[13].

If you're finding yourself in a place and saying, 'I can't worship here', then you probably can't worship anywhere else either – because worship has nothing to do with places. As Jesus once said to a woman who was both a victim and perpetrator of worship boundaries, *'The time is coming when it will no longer matter whether you worship the Father here or in Jerusalem... the time is coming and is already here when true worshipers will worship the Father in spirit and in truth'*[14].

Again, when I talk about worship I'm not talking about singing, or about praising God with happy songs when we don't feel happy.

I'm talking about aiming to honour God in everything we say and do, wherever we find ourselves. Worship has everything to do with what we do have and nothing to do with what we don't! Just give to God what belongs to Him.

> 'And whatever you do or say, let it be as a representative of the Lord Jesus, all the while giving thanks through him to God the Father'[15]

MINE

But what is God's? Is everything His?

And even if the answer to the above is 'yes' (which I strongly suspect it is), not everything is mine to give. It would be easy to give God what isn't mine – but it's not for me to take what is Caesar's and give it to God. I am only responsible for what is mine to give, that's the real exclusivity of worship. This is why, within the Old Testament, King David insists on buying a threshing floor from a man named Araunah saying, 'I cannot take what is yours and give it to the LORD. I will not offer a burnt offering that has cost me nothing!'[16].

Like all expressions of love, worship is both corporate and personal.

When I think about it, there's really only one thing that is in my control to give – myself, the totality of my life. But, and I have to be honest here, I do struggle with this; I find myself in a constant battle with an ego that wants the story to be all about me. C.S. Lewis puts his finger right on this one, when he says the following:

> 'We try, when we wake, to lay the new day at God's feet; before we have finished shaving, it becomes our day and God's share in it is felt as a tribute which we must pay out of 'our own' pocket, a deduction from the time which ought, we feel, to be 'our own'[17]

I feel this tension in my own life, but I'm aware that this is what true love does – it gives itself, not roses or chocolates, but being. When love is expressed through worship, it's always sacrificial – it seeks to allow its identity to be the container for the image of another.

What keeps me from making this step is my pride, because I feel that it is my time, my home, it is my job. If my life is to look like anybody, then it should be me, after all, I've expended a lot of energy on my identity over the years. I am mine.

But this is naive of me, as there's an awful lot that I haven't been responsible for, a host of things that I had no choice about, but that were all formative to who I am and who I'm becoming. I didn't choose the genes I would get. I didn't choose the parents or siblings, or the kind of home that I would grow up with. I had no control over many of the responses others would have towards me. I didn't pick the country and economy I would be raised up in, which to a large degree determined the opportunities that would be made readily available to me – and if we go further I certainly didn't choose this planet. I didn't really choose my wife – she also had to choose me. I didn't choose sickness or ill-health. I had no say in what my children would be born like, yeah I was involved in the transmission of twenty-three of their chromosomes, but the potential results of that are mind-boggling, which again affects how I am as a dad... We could go on, but I think the point is made. I'm not the 'self-made' man I sometimes delude myself into thinking that I am. Every day of my life, more and more material is given to me to construct an altar with, but I often find that I have no choice over what that material is or who/what may borrow some of it.

My sense of pride is distorted, because my perspective isn't right. To once again borrow the words of someone more articulate, A.J. Jacobs, who in his fantastic book *The Year of Living Biblically*, makes the following observation about the reason for worship: '*I have my head bowed and my eyes closed. I'm trying to pray, but my mind is wandering. I can't settle it down. It wanders over to an esquire article I just wrote. It wasn't half bad, I think to myself. I liked that turn of phrase in the first paragraph.*

And then I am hit with a realisation. And hit is the right word – it felt like a punch to my stomach. Here I am being prideful about creating an article in a midsize American magazine. But God – if He exists – He created the world. He created flamingos and supernovas and geysers and beetles and the stones for these steps I'm sitting on. "Praise the Lord," I say out loud. I'd always found the praising-God parts of the Bible and my prayer books awkward. The sentences about the all-powerful, almighty, all-knowing, the host of hosts, He who has greatness beyond our comprehension. I'm not used to talking like that. It's over the top. I'm used to understatement and hedging and irony. And why would God need to be praised in the first place? God shouldn't be insecure. He's the ultimate being. Now I can sort of see why. It's not for him. It's for us. It takes you out of yourself and your prideful little brain'[18]

I love that in the story of the book of Genesis, once humanity is formed, the first morning that mankind gets to experience is the day of Sabbath. The day of rest. The day of appreciation. And that one of the first commandments they are given by the Creator is, 'Look!'[19].

It's almost as if God is saying, 'Before you go rushing into this life, and making things and doing *your* thing, just stop, pause, look around, and take it all in. Get an appreciation of what came before you and what it was that put it there – actually, get a proper perspective of what it is that made *you*, you!' Again, referring back to the infamous Ten Commandments, I don't think it's just a coincidence that after the call for us to remember that the story is about God, and after the words that call us to bear His image, there then comes the instruction to keep the practice of Sabbath.

'Look!' – To express love through worship is impossible without that one little act. To still seek God after discovering Him may be a love paradox of the soul, as A.W. Tozer reminds us; but to earnestly continue to perceive God and make Him perceivable, is the quintessence of worship.

BROKEN MIRROR

As I mentioned earlier, Paul the Apostle reminds us in his second letter to the church at Corinth that we are like mirrors that are to reflect the glory of God. However, the mirror of humanity is fractured. Regardless of whether we read the story in Genesis as historical or parabolic, in humanity's grasping to be as God, in wanting ourselves to be the focus, we fell and cracked. We struggle to see the image of the divine in the world today. Although it isn't fully lost, if we took the time to focus on the reflections contained within the shards, instead of just focusing on the whole shattered mess, we would notice something.

Personally, I'm no better than the whole – my own shard is stained and scarred. Even as a follower of Jesus, I have my struggles. I'm not the perfect picture. I'm learning, I'm giving myself to the journey of discipleship, I'm spending time in the sanctuary – but if you just look at me, you won't get a true image. What you might actually get is more like what you would expect to see in a carnival 'hall of mirrors' – not a true impression of the divine, but more of a disproportional funfair caricature.

This is why no one person should be our *image* of God; they will eventually disappoint you, and if they don't, then I worry that the picture of God you'll be given won't be a hundred percent accurate. The image needs to be more corporate. But even this isn't enough to repair the problem.

God in his wisdom foresaw this problem. And so, the God who calls us to bear His image came and bore ours. As Paul writes:

> 'Christ is the visible image of the invisible God. He existed before God made anything at all and is supreme over all creation. Christ is the one through whom God created everything in heaven and earth. He made the things we can see and the things we can't see – kings, kingdoms, rulers, and authorities. Everything has been created through him and for him. He existed before everything else began, and he holds all creation together.

Christ is the head of the Church, which is his body.
He is the first of all who will rise from the dead, so he is
first in everything. For God in all his fullness was pleased
to live in Christ, and by him God reconciled everything in
heaven and earth by the means of his blood on the cross' [20]

Jesus is the IKON of God. Through Christ, God has given us a symbol that communicates across all time and space, a symbol that can be understood regardless of the context. The worship that Jesus offered was perfect. When we watch Jesus, we observe God; God among the broken, God among the weary, God among the outcast and the socially unacceptable – God ministering to the shattered mirrors of humanity.

If you want to see God – look at Jesus. He's the reference point. But not only does Jesus show us what God looks like, He speaks to us about what humanity should look like.

We would fight, throwing off God's image, to get it engraved on to something else. But Jesus, taking yet another symbol of humanity's domination, allows Himself to be engraved. Taking a symbol of power, a token of death and punishment, through His submission and surrender Jesus converts it into a symbol of hope.

'The leading Jews are going to hand over to Caesar not only the coin that bears his image, and his false title 'son of God', but the human being who truly bears God's image, and who truly bears that title. But, in that act, they are unwittingly offering to God the one stamped with the mark of self-giving love. The cross itself is taken up into both Caesar's purposes and God's: Caesar's favourite weapon, the cross, becomes God's chosen instrument of salvation.' [21]

Through His death and His resurrection, Jesus brings us into the mosaic of His body. God becomes the grout between our brokenness, and works to reform us into the image He so desires.

DO THIS...

Prior to the above events, Jesus finds Himself sharing a meal with His closest followers. It's famously known as 'The Last Supper', and during it there comes the point when Jesus takes some bread and some wine and presents a new symbol to His friends.

Just bread, just wine, normal everyday things, but Jesus takes them and does something that makes them containers for something else.

As they pass the emblems around the table, over the sounds of ripping bread and slurping wine, above the smell of fresh-baked grain and mixed into the tones of the fruit of the vine, Jesus' voice declares, 'Do this in remembrance of me...'

I'm sure that as the disciples ate and drank on that first occasion, that it was all still *just* bread and wine. But after the crucifixion, in the weeks and years that followed, I wonder what thoughts and feelings leaked out of those simple containers?

The Eucharist, Communion, 'the love feast', still holds special significance for the church today. These symbols are still resonating with us, as we too, discover Jesus. We take these symbols and remember the breaking of His flesh, and the flowing of His blood. They are symbols, along with others, which are central to our identity.

But I want to extend the imagery, and I don't mean to do so in any heretical way, but if we can take normal things like bread and wine and remember Jesus, then why not everything else? By taking my life, and giving to God all that is His, then the *this* in Jesus' words carries the potential to become anything and everything.

'Do *family* in remembrance of me...'
    'Do *work* in remembrance of me...'
        'Do *gardening* in remembrance of me...'
            'Do *Glastonbury* in remembrance of me...'

Do life in remembrance of Jesus...

I don't just want to exist. I long for my life to speak of Him. I long for our life together to speak of Him.

We have a saying in our church community, although I wouldn't go as far as to say it's unique to us, but it goes something like this – 'Love God, love people and do what you like'.

It's a dangerous saying, I know. But if we truly love God, then in everything we do, we will want to do it with the agenda to evoke memories of Him, helping people to once again sense God. I don't believe people are absent of a knowledge of God. Deep down, it's in there; hidden away, maybe forgotten. But what if the divine music of our lives can somehow help bring those long-forgotten words back to the lips of others?[22]

> *'Give thanks to the Lord and proclaim his greatness. Let the whole world know what he has done. Sing to him; yes, sing his praises. Tell everyone about his wonderful deeds. Exult in his holy name; rejoice, you who worship the Lord. Search for the Lord and for his strength; continually seek him. Remember the wonders he has performed, his miracles, and the rulings he has given.' –* 1 Chronicles 16:8-12 (NLT)

> *'So whatever you eat or drink, or whatever you do, do it all for the glory of God' –* 1 Corinthians 10:31 (NLT)

EXPRESSED THROUGH **SABBATH**

'You don't have to go, you know?'
Stephanie Sherwin[1]

TEARS & TOAST

Sandwiched between the expletives that bubbled up and exploded every three to four minutes were also tears, cries of desperation, thumping of the car dashboard, and deep, erratic intakes of breath. Throughout the thirty minute episode, the volume had been switching frantically from shouting and mumbling, to just empty lip movements – all in the hope that I could somehow vomit out the agony that was the cause of so much inner turmoil towards a God who I felt had abandoned me.

This was me – sat in our little *Fiat Seicento* on the drive of our home, at ten o'clock on a Wednesday evening in April 2010 – in the midst of a breakdown.

When I say breakdown, I'm not talking about the car. It was me who was falling to pieces.

Of course, I didn't know it then. I had no idea what was taking place or why I'd suddenly become so unable to prevent the release of all this emotion.

Raw emotion too, the unedited stuff, the things my usual calmness allowed me to censor. I sat in that car filled with anger – scary anger – and utter confusion. I was frustrated and hurt, exhausted, stressed, and severely, severely depressed. But there I sat, venting my rage, while God silently listened.

I didn't want to go into our home. I didn't want to see anyone, not even Steph – who had been worried and upset for the past five hours about my absence. All she had heard from me during that time was a text message as I left work saying, 'I can't do it anymore... I'm quitting... I can't go on'.

After sending that text I'd driven for an hour to a secluded spot I favoured as a teenager, in an attempt to escape the 'noise' of life around me and to clear my head. It didn't work though. When I'd eventually arrived at seclusion, I discovered that I couldn't filter my thoughts – I was unable to stop my mind racing back and forth and sideways. I'd brought the 'noise' with me, and all the "holding it in" methods I'd developed in past experience wouldn't silence it – the pep talks, the self-encouragement, declaring scripture, the dismissing and diminishing of what was happening – as much as I tried, I wasn't able to push my feelings back into the proverbial wardrobe. And the tighter I clung in trying to keep-it-together the more my mind seemed to ooze through my grasp on reality.

The seclusion was nice, but it had only amplified my distress and despair – it was as if the emptiness of the environment had provided a cave to return the echo. I couldn't stay – it was uncomfortable hearing myself – plus, after an hour since arriving, my appetite had also started to vie for attention. So, I set off once more in my search for sanity, but this time I wanted it with a side order of sustenance.

I've never felt as alone as I did while I sat there, in that supermarket chain café, eating cheese toasties and side salad with hands that wouldn't stop shaking. It wasn't that I'd never eaten on my own before – I had. But my sense of isolation was being nurtured by watching those around me. Through the café windows I could see people packing their "weekly-big-shop" into the back of their cars; some laughed together and took their time, others rushed about with their minds full of further commitments. Scattered around me, marooned from me on their own tables, other people shared conversations about life, and families, and work, and TV shows... Everyone else seemed to be 'getting on with *it'*, still progressing, happy with the rate of flow. Was I the only one who had 'stalled'? Was I the only one struggling to keep pace?

My phone began vibrating on the table top as text messages and phone calls (which I purposefully avoided answering) started coming through. Word had now gotten out about my being AWOL – 'Are you ok?', 'Hey buddy, do you want to talk?', 'Praying for you...', at which point I wanted to scream and throw something (my phone being the number one candidate), but it wasn't just the munchies that had brought me to a café. I was hoping that a public space might help to psychologically suppress whatever it was I was struggling with. I'd thought that maybe my sense of vanity would restrain me from 'losing it' altogether – not fully accepting that I already was 'losing it'. I already looked peculiar – sitting there, alone, shaking as I shovelled grilled bread into the mouth of my ill-looking face.

I finished my food and figured it was time to move on again. But I couldn't go home like this. I needed to talk, about anything really – anything except this. I just wanted to laugh and be distracted, so I decided to visit my brother Colin; not really appreciating how odd it is to turn up on your brother's doorstep at eight in the evening of a work night, unannounced, alone, without wife and children, and miles from home. He welcomed me in, made me a brew, shared pleasantries and invited me to join him on his *Xbox* marathon. Eventually though, he tackled the elephant in the room – 'So, why are you here, what's up?'

I began to open up and share about my disappointments, my fatigue, my sadness (thanks for listening bro). But I did so in a guarded way, without giving too much away.

You know what I mean by this, don't you? Someone asks you how you are, and you tell them, but in a *reserved* way – speaking of our feelings, while at the same time holding those feelings back, so they're never actually seen?

Colin sat there listening, while simultaneously focusing on his current mission to upgrade a level status. Occasionally he prodded me with further questions and shared his opinions, and by the end of the visit I did somehow seem a bit better, things felt ok – and I wondered if I had once again managed to keep the illusion alive. In the hope that I had, I began the journey home.

Home.

There's no place like it for me, it's the place where I can just *be*. It's that natural environment where I cease to pretend, where masks are removed and veils are lifted.

So, inevitably, that's where the illusion broke. As I parked the car and closed our gates behind me, I could feel the anxiety surging in me once again, but there was no stopping it this time. I quickly got back into my car, and closed the door in time for the sticky-tape-illusion of a patch-job that I'd used to seal the wardrobe doors with, to snap – and out it all came, in a torrent of language and tears and groans.

It wasn't pleasant. And I am sure our *Seicento* wasn't the best at providing sound insulation – I have no idea who heard me that night. But there I sat for thirty minutes, outpouring until I felt physically weakened.

Eventually, I made my way back into the house. Exhausted and silent, I walked past Steph, up the stairs of our home, past the rooms where our two boys peacefully slept, and climbed into bed. And there, while still shaking and mumbling, I fell asleep.

INSANE

I don't know what insane is meant to look like. The movies always seem to portray it in obvious ways, like it's clearly visible; you can spot the people who are nuts – they wear clothes that don't match; they have strange mannerisms and speak in fluctuating pitches during sentences. 'Mad' people also seem to have hair styles that match their behaviour, shooting out from the top of their heads at peculiar, uncouth angles.

But honestly, abnormal is not that easy to spot – its camouflage is a lot more subtle.

Insanity is often that small internal voice that convinces you to 'suck it in, it'll be ok, just get through another day, put the mask back on... *act* normal, because that's what *normal* is'.

It's extremely persuasive, and it certainly had me convinced the morning after. I woke up, and regardless of the 'greyness' (as I now call it) that swamped me, I proceeded, in a *Walking Dead* kind of fashion, getting washed, dressed and ready for work.

I can't have been more than two footsteps away from our back-door, when Steph said a handful of words that changed my world. Words that somehow found me in the mist I was engulfed by. Words, which left unspoken, would have permitted me to walk into a day's events that I cannot, and do not want to begin to fathom. Words that, as I look back from the clarity I presently occupy, God had been saying to me for years prior but I hadn't heeded:

'You don't have to go, you know?'

Those words seized me. I stopped. I started to shake. The tears started to run down my face again, and in a wobbly fashion I made my way back into the house, stumbled upstairs, climbed back into bed (fully clothed) and wept, and shook, and slept, and wept...

That bed became an incubator for me as the breakdown ran its course, as I finally gave in and let go. A year-long process dotted with episodes like the one in the car. It's a chapter of my life that has left its scars – but it wasn't the breakdown that inflicted the wounds – it was actually a process that had begun to acknowledge them and heal them.

What had led to all of this? Well, simply put, a broken church window and an email!

That's not quite true. The truth is more layered than that. The window and the email were just something and nothing, but unfortunately they were the 'straws that broke the camel's back'. The reality was that I was overworked, I was doing too much. I had a full-time job, a young family and was pastoring a small church. My week was stupid. I only had one or two weeknights free each week – and if there wasn't some 'emergency' to solve, or a phone call to make, then I was usually spending extra time prepping sermons or trying to think ahead.

Needless to say, this doesn't make for a great relationship with your partner in life. But I became aware of this, and the solution I developed, in the year or so leading up to my breakdown, was to push the prep and thinking to after bedtime – burning the midnight oil became the norm. And on those nights when I did spend an evening with Steph, I wasn't really present, even though I tried.

Eventually I hit a stage when even the normal engagements in life were inconvenient – fun, the weekly big-shop, washing the pots, holidays, reading bedtime stories to the kids, relationships... Then there's the unexpected stuff in life – the child illnesses, the hospital appointments, the car's MOT failure, house maintenance... the stuff that just turns up to join the party!

And then the working day gets longer, things begin to get busier in the world of employment – you move up a level, which usually translates to 'you're spread thinner' – and the more pressure you carry, the later you work, which dominoes everything else along. I can remember at least more than once staying up until three in the morning prepping, only to get up at seven, to go to work, to then get home, to spend some rushed time with my family, to then stay up prepping and planning and studying some more...

(And I haven't even got the time to mention all the other perceived *needs* that I never got round to looking at, those things that kept stacking up in the background. Nor do I have the time to discuss the weight of other people's demands and expectations...)

In hindsight, it's not a great sign when you begin to sweat a little when the phone rings. It's not a good marker in life when you begin to feel guilty about watching a movie with your wife or going to a park with your kids, because you feel, or you are told, that there are other things that *need* your attention. It's not healthy when all it takes to drain the colour from your face, in such a rapid and drastic fashion that a fellow work colleague comments on it, is a broken window and an email about a simple, easy to rectify issue.

ˈwouʞ ı ˈuʍop ǝpısdn sˌʇı

But, underpinning all of this behaviour was one little ideal – an insane ideal that had been driven into my head via leadership conferences, books and media; an ideal that the culture around me self-perpetuates, and celebrates, and salivates over – "success".

FEAR

I'm led to believe that the biggest fear in the world is Arachnophobia, the fear of spiders. And even though I can see the reasoning for this – especially when it concerns hairy-legged-bathtub-lounging arachnids with abdomens bigger than my son's fingernails – I don't agree with the statistics.

From what I've observed and what I've experienced, I think for many people in the West, our largest fear is becoming a *nobody*!

It consumes our culture, so much so that I don't really need to give any examples – to some degree, you'll probably already sense it too. But sadly, it feels that this fear has also permeated some streams within the church. It seems that every conference I go to, especially leadership conferences, have the main-headlining-agenda of 'success' – *building successful churches... having 'successful Sundays'... being a successful leader... becoming a more successful you* (yes, you're right, I need to pick some better conferences). From what I understand, the emphasis gets heavily placed on the need for every individual to have 'a dream', or to have 'a vision', and that a lot of this conversation is packaged in a marketing language that tries to disguise itself as 'faith', but its tone is still the DIY mantras of *'do more'*, *'work harder'*, *'accomplish'*...

To be clear, I don't have an issue with placing goals in our worlds – our societies are not free of pain, suffering and injustice – there are things that we should be working towards. Neither am I saying that it's a bad thing to 'have a dream' (although, I always want to sing that song from *Disney's Tangled* when I hear those words put together). And please don't mistake me for being gullible; I understand the necessity of work, and yes, I know that following Jesus is a life characterised by our actions and expressions (hence this book), so neither am I negating a certain need to *do*.

But, and this is a big but, why does it often feel like we western Christians are so worn out? Why do some Christians I meet, admittedly in private conversation, suffer from identity crisis's predominantly rooted in comparisons to other Christians? Why are a good number of church leaders' (and other people's) 'dreams/visions', often just another way to disguise demands? Why does it feel like we are, as humans, entertained/driven/motivated, but in turn, exhausted and fed up by an infatuation to attain and achieve? Why are things like discipleship, church growth and church planting, sometimes presented in ways that feel like a large-scale religious version of *Monopoly*?

I wonder if some areas of western Christianity, like the man rescued from the pool of Bethesda, are still trapped by the water's allure – where the adherents of those streams, once driven by the materialism, consumerism and individualist dreams of the world around us, were rescued by Christ, only to find their redemption 'sabotaged' by religious leaders telling us we still need more. We are saved from the rat-race, but I meet so many who have been suckered into just another Christian alternative of the world around us, and not the Kingdom of God.

Jesus said, 'Come to me, all you who are weary and carry heavy burdens, and I will give you rest'[2] – and yet, in a good number of evangelical churches, following Jesus doesn't look restful, it's clothed like a rigorous *Insanity* style workout. There's a sort of pressure to perform.

And that's not just the leader's expectations of their congregations; it's also vice-versa.

Maybe it's just me who sees it this way, and these paragraphs are just some outworking of my own personal 'demons' and negativity, or my perception has warped because of my own self-induced scars. Well, that could be true. If that is the case, then please forgive me – feel free to skip this chapter and carry on without having to entertain my personal vent. But I detect, at least I hope, that it isn't just me who senses this problem.

Am I the only one who is troubled by this?

Am I the only one who feels that in some churches/movements (I must stress – not all!), we have become so *success/identity* driven that faith isn't about having faith in Jesus anymore; it sounds more like some self-help therapeutic tendency, where the concept of faith seems to be rooted in an individual's own capability to advance? And underlying all of that 'faith-talk' isn't love, or actual biblical faith, but actually fear, a fear that the expositors of this brand of 'faith' purposely exploit – a fear of being forgotten, a fear of being overlooked, a fear of not achieving, a fear of our personal dreams not coming to fruition, a fear of not leaving some kind of legacy... a fear of becoming 'no one'.

Instead of being *Christocentric*, our Christianity (our world even) is in danger of being *Egocentric*.[3]

We are in desperate need of the reality check that comes through the loving expression of Sabbath.

COUNTING BRICKS

The fourth commandment states, 'Remember to observe the Sabbath...'[4] and can be found within both the Old Testament books of Exodus and Deuteronomy. However, if you give both of these passages a read you'll soon come to notice that there exists a difference between the texts, a difference that lies in the motivation behind the instruction – a purposeful modification due to a forty-year generation gap.

In Exodus, the recently freed slaves of Egypt are gathered around the 'Mountain of God' (Sinai), while their liberator – Moses – shares of his encounter with their Creator. These people are still fresh from the escape, and would have had no problems recalling the hardships they've had to endure in Egypt, producing the gruelling quota of progresses' building blocks.

The regime that dominated them was one driven by the attainment of wealth and power, a system that necessitated they work every day of the week in order to manufacture mud bricks that would facilitate the construction of places to house the nation's mammon (in this case grain). In Egypt, every day consisted of counting – the slaves worked tirelessly to achieve the quantities which their foremen had to monitor, which the Pharaoh oversaw, and which the insatiable gods demanded. Every stratum of this system was dictated to by the drive to produce, and to produce to such an extent that surplus was created – but the work continued. For generations this economy has perpetuated, it's the 'norm', a 'status quo' that is accepted and embraced by all – there is no rest in Egypt.

These slaves had been born and bound into a culture of relentless production for so long that they had probably become persuaded of this means and meaning of living. Maybe their unceasing work for seven days had stained their minds with strange ideas of what existence was about and how it needed to be maintained. Because of this, as Moses gives what we now call the Ten Commandments to this generation, he feels the need to remind them of the 'rhythm of God's work'. So coupled with the command of Sabbath, Moses also reminds the people of the creation account – in six days God made *everything that was needed*, then He took a day off. God worked, but then He sat back to enjoy what He had made.

That story would have presented a deeply cultural contradiction to these people. As Walter Bruggemann puts it in his brilliant book *Sabbath as Resistance*,

'That divine rest on the seventh day of creation has made clear (a) that YHWH is not a workaholic, (b) that YHWH is not anxious about the full functioning of creation, and (c) that the well-being of creation does not depend on endless work. This performance and exhibit of divine rest thus characterize the God of creation, creation itself, and the creatures made in the image of a resting God... Indeed, such divine rest serves to delegitimate and dismantle the endless restlessness sanctioned by the other gods and enacted by their adherents'[5]

In the Exodus account, Moses takes the time to stress to the fledgling Hebrew nation that the one true God's mandate for creation is different from the oppressive and megalomaniac 'dream' of the Egyptian gods. Under God, you work, yes, but you also rest and receive and express, and make a practice of this.

Try to imagine what that freed nation felt as it woke for its first Sabbath and realised it didn't *need* to go to work. I wonder how many nights it took them to get into the practice of going to sleep without the need of counting bricks?

Alternatively, the Deuteronomy generation of Hebrews, with the exceptions of the 'ones and twos', knew nothing of the slavery of Egypt first-hand. They have only known the provision of God in the wilderness through manna, quails, water and sandals that don't wear down... they don't need reminding of God's creative acts, so Moses doesn't remind them of this like he does with the Sinai pilgrims.

However, for this new generation, there is the danger that they have never really known the responsibility to provide. When Moses delivers these words, this forty-year-old nation is getting ready to cross the Jordan River into a land of their own. And once they do cross over that watery border, that miraculous provision of manna and 'indestructible flip-flops' will eventually come to an end.

They will have to produce, and build, and farm, and work... which is good, but it can get addictive building a nation. When constructing an empire 'dreams' can landslide into 'demands'. With a production mindset, it's easy to become possessed by materialism and consumerism; if unchecked the appetite for more can grow ravenous, the need to *achieve* and *accomplish* and *perform* and *possess* can grow out of control. When this happens we can begin to see ourselves, and those around us, as purely means to our success agenda; people become viewed as commodities – either 'cogs' or 'spanners' within the machine of productivity. With imperial thinking, it's tempting to look at the other nations we share our borders with and begin to want what they have. Existence can rapidly diminish to simply another definition of 'working/moving towards...', being successful becomes a matter of comparison with your neighbour, and your identity starts to be shaped by what you, yourself, have *or* haven't achieved.

To the Deuteronomy generation, Moses needs to give them a reminder that they, their people, were once slaves under a system obsessed with empire, and that they need to recall that this preoccupation was so choking that it was only through the intervention of God's power that they had been delivered from it – they certainly couldn't *work* or *attain* their way to freedom.

Both the Exodus and Deuteronomy motivation behind the Sabbath are proclaimed as being '...why the LORD your God has commanded you to observe the Sabbath day'[6]. Well, which is correct? – In short, both. They are both different sides of the same coin, a reminder that '...life is more than food, and the body more than clothing'[7] (all things that have to be produced); life does not need to be defined by production and attaining – some things are given. 'Without Sabbath', Moses is saying, 'you could end up building another regime like that of Egypt!'

The point is hammered home in each case by the injunction to '*Remember* to observe...' At our most exploited and exhausted, at our most active and covetous, we are most prone to forget the alternative, or have it withheld from us – an alternative that Sabbath causes us to consider. Again, to quote Walter Brueggemann,

> 'The alternative on offer is that awareness and practice of the claim that we are situated on the receiving end of the gifts of God. To be so situated is a staggering option, because we are accustomed to being on the initiating end of all things'[8]

> 'Sabbath is not simply a pause... Sabbath is an invitation to receptivity, an acknowledgement that what is needed is given and need not be seized'[9]

I'm not sure how you measure your progression in life. Maybe, for some of us, we're counting our achievements – the things we have produced, the things we have built?

There's that old saying that I am well used to hearing, 'If at first you don't succeed, try, try again'. I don't doubt the validity of this in the right circumstance. But with our current context in mind, I decided for myself a few years back to change this saying around – 'If at first you don't succeed, then maybe you have the wrong idea of success, or you're using the wrong standard of measuring it'.

I wonder, are we counting blessings, or are we counting bricks?

If we really consider the above, then we will come to the realisation that Sabbath is not a law to obey – it's not another thing to do, it's not another stepping stone to our version of success – but it's a grace to enjoy. To practise Sabbath is to put down our agenda of *work* and *performance* and to revel in God's work. It's the time to sample, to taste and to discover creation. Sabbath is a challenge to our do-it-yourself existence. Little wonder it occupies the largest word count in the Ten Commandments.

MONOPOLY

'Technical civilization is man's conquest of space. It is a triumph frequently achieved by sacrificing an essential ingredient of existence, namely time. In technical civilization, we expend time to gain space. To enhance our power in the world of space is our main objective. Yet to have more does not mean to be more. The power we attain in the world of space terminates abruptly at the borderline of time. But time is the heart of existence... There is a realm of time where the goal is not to have but to be, not to own but to give, not to control but to share, not to subdue but to be in accord. Life goes wrong when the control of space, the acquisition of things of space, becomes our sole concern.'[10]

You've got to appreciate the insight that the Jewish scholar Abraham Joshua Heschel gives in the quote above; it says it rather nicely, to say the least. For myself, I liken it to the game *Monopoly*.

Most of us will know how the board game *Monopoly* works. We understand its aim and we play by its rules (although some of us add rules that don't exist in the official *Monopoly* rule book – like placing all the monies paid in taxes and repairs in the centre of the board, to be scooped up by whoever lands next on the 'free-parking' square). So please don't misunderstand what I am about to say – I don't have an issue with the game itself, I've played it many times and I even own a copy, although it is *The Simpsons* version.

But has the game's goal, become our real-life goal?

In *Monopoly* everyone's fighting and outbidding each other for space, because having space, and controlling space, and building things in space, is what the game is all about. And we don't just want any space, we're only accepting of *Old Kent* Road if it helps us in our striving for *Mayfair* (or the *Tire Yard* and *Mr Burn's Manor*, in the version we possess).

You see, in the game, you have to possess and build, you have to speculate in order to accumulate, you have to conquer and bankrupt the competition. The game's about dominating as much as we can in order to be the one person who out survives everyone else. It's 'dog eat dog' as the saying goes. There's no room for second place.

For some, life's aim is not much different than Monopoly's – except instead of paper currency, they spend *time* in order to dominate the board. For others, this isn't the goal, but we still feel trapped in the game, being used as the pieces that are caught in the endless cycle of passing *go*.

I'm conscious, as I write, that I live in an affluent country, that my family and I are fortunate to be a part of that 1-2% of humanity's wealthiest – but what about the rest, because there's a big gap between us and them when it comes to dominating the board? Some would say, 'They could become like us if they too would aim to dominate space, to advance technologically'. But those other people groups, who have to live hand to mouth each day, have, in the main, become stripped of their resources and land at the hands of other countries and individuals because of that same drive for progress. Humanity's desire to win the game has raped and pillaged creation, and left its STIs of war, greed and famine all over our ecology and societies. To dominate space is not the cure to its own self-inflicted diseases.

I'm reminded of the 'Ghost of Christmas Present's' warning to Mr Ebenezer Scrooge in Charles Dickens' classic *A Christmas Carol*. As the spectre draws back his robes to reveal the *'wretched, abject, frightful, hideous, miserable'* forms of a boy and girl – the offspring of mankind – he warns Scrooge to beware of them, not the children themselves, but the things that have produced and prolonged their condition – *ignorance* and *want*. Yet, despite Dickens' powerful narrative, mankind is still denying the label written across the boy's brow and slandering those who take the time to spell it out to us.

Even on our own affluent shores, our striving to survive and develop is costing us in other ways. Families are stretched in their time together, the effects of debt are chipping away at communities, and stress related illnesses are on the increase. According to a BBC News article I read recently, seventy million working hours were lost last year alone (2013-2014) because of mental illness. Mental illness, the report stated, costs the economy between £70bn and £100bn in lost productivity, benefit payments and absence from work'[11]. That's a sobering and saddening statistic – what makes it more saddening for me personally, is that the only way we can measure the effects of mental illness is in the *loss* of working hours and *productivity* (talk about counting bricks!).

Let's be honest, we live in a culture where it looks good to be busy and we can be deeply suspicious of those who aren't.

In twenty-first century western life, *rest* is treated like a natural version of *Red Bull*. We do take it, occasionally, but often it's only as a means to guarantee greater productivity.

Please understand, I'm not criticising anybody. I know that there will be many people who will share these concerns but, like myself, will often feel trapped in thinking that this is how the game must be played. But as a victim of the game I have to ask, is our 'progress for progress sake' actually progressive? Is our culture really all that different from that of Egypt?

In our longing to feel alive, has humanity indoctrinated itself with the mistaken ideas that to exist is to survive, to develop is to compete, and to experience is to consume?

We need rest like we need oxygen, and *real* rest – not the energy drink version. 'We work to live' is what I'm constantly told – but am I the only one who feels that there is too little time left in our expenditure to actually practise living?

To practise Sabbath is to love ourselves enough, and those around us, to give ourselves a day off from playing the game.

TIME KEEPING

In his book *The Sabbath*, from which the above quote is taken, Heschel notes that within the creation account of Genesis, at the end of each creative day, God declares all he has made as 'good', and at the end of the sixth day God declares all creation as 'very good', but it is only the Sabbath – a 'time' not a 'thing in space' – that God declares as being 'holy'.

Moses also reminds us of this; as he gives the commandments, he declares that the Sabbath is to be observed by keeping it holy.

But how?

I'm from a different generation to some when it comes to 'keeping the faith' – I'm still pretty much the new kid on the block. But I hear the stories about how 'The Lord's Day' was kept – with its rules of 'do nots' and 'can dos'; I've even been privy to my forbears' conversations about which day actually is 'the Lord's'.

But I need you to understand that the focus of my writing here is not to tilt us towards a particular day out of the seven. I am not writing this as a treatise against our nation's supermarkets being open seven days a week. My aim is not to stop people watching *Match of the Day* when they come home from church on a Sunday evening (so, my good friend Paul needn't panic).

I'm not too concerned with those things – maybe I should be?

However, I am concerned about our work-life balance.

In our rat-race, success driven culture – is there room for a day off, when we stop counting bricks, when we protest against passing *go* and we just say, 'Stop'? I don't really care if that's a Sunday, or the actual Sabbath day of Saturday – it could be a Wednesday or a Monday (I wish!).

Can we afford to allow one seventh of our existence to not be dominated with egocentric, nationalistic or consumeristic pursuits? Do we have the time to just enjoy time, instead of spending it, when we celebrate and express eternity, and not fashion, when we can marvel at creation as a living system, and not exploit it like an organic factory? Could that be what it means to keep the Sabbath holy?

Heschel suggests,

> 'This, then, is the answer to the problems of civilization: not to flee from the realm of space; to work with things of space but to be in love with eternity'[12]

Without Sabbath, in *our* felt need to attain and accomplish we run the risk of forfeiting what really makes us, us. In trying to be, we cease to be. In gaining the world, we risk losing our grip on the divine reality.

> 'We labor and fret for a small gain, while loss of the soul is forgotten and scarcely ever returns to mind. That which is of little or no value claims our attention, whereas that which is of highest necessity is neglected – all because man gives himself wholly to outward things. And unless he withdraws himself quickly, he willingly lies immersed in externals'[13]

I believe Jesus kept the Sabbath well. I believe He kept it holy. I believe He lavished in, and was lavish with, eternity – even while He continued to work in space.

IT *IS* FINISHED!

If you can remember the story from the first chapter of this book – the story of the man and the pool, in John chapter 5 – then please also note that Jesus did this miracle on the Sabbath.

And that upset people.

A lot.

In the verses that follow the miracle, Jesus gets harassed by some of the Jewish leaders for breaking the rules of the Sabbath, man-made rules, like the extra rules in *Monopoly*, which dictated how the Sabbath should be kept. But Jesus' simple, yet extremely controversial alibi for breaking those 'rules' was, '*My Father never stops working, so why should I?*'[14]

This wasn't a one-time offence for Jesus – there are numerous other occasions when He 'breaks the Sabbath rules'. He was always going around doing good, when others thought he should be doing nothing[15].

Jesus' activity on the Sabbath upset people, well, some people. Some people absolutely loved and celebrated Jesus' work on the Sabbath days – they were usually the broken people that He repaired, the people that society labelled the 'spanners' in the works – those that the well-oiled production machine of 'space domination' has no place for. Still, others deeply resented what Jesus was doing and were appalled by Jesus' tinkering with the mechanism. Jesus upset them, because He upset their thinking about Sabbath.

For Jesus it was a day for *doing* good; for continuing to enjoy and to express the Father's eternal intent for a fully-functioning harmonious creation. For Him, the Sabbath was a celebration of being alive.

However, for the legalists who objected to Jesus' work, the Sabbath had slid from a day for resting in, enjoying and expressing God's creative acts; it had become just another way of trying to *attain* and *accomplish*. In this sense, they themselves were working, via the observance and enforcement of man-made rules in order to gain the approval of God – and by gaining the approval of God, they hoped to then receive the Kingdom, one that would come and rival the other kingdoms, one that would enter the contest and remove the competition.

But God's Kingdom is not interested in contest. The Kingdom's manifesto doesn't read like the imperial agenda of other nations – the famous *Sermon on the Mount* (*The Beatitudes*, Matthew 5) doesn't adopt the same strategies as most political parties. God's Kingdom does not intend to be in competition with the world's empires, it's subversive to the rules of how empires are formed; it doesn't seek to remove and annihilate the opposition, it seeks to bless them and revolutionise them.

For the legalists, the pursuit is to dominate space. Their mindset is still performance-driven. But for Jesus, the focus was on eternity's activity within the present reality. Jesus' mindset was expression.

Jesus' practice of Sabbath was not a challenge to activity, but the purpose and objective behind our activity. Jesus says that 'God is always working!' If this is the case, then the Sabbath is not the rejection of all work, just the work that seeks to play religious *Monopoly*.

So when Genesis tells us that God rested, this doesn't necessarily need to be interpreted as 'God doing nothing' – He celebrated with His creation.

Just in case you might be thinking that I'm anti-business, I'm not; Sabbath is not a call to abandon your job, or to get out of mowing the lawn, or a rule book that says what you can and cannot do on a particular day. Sabbath is a protest against the notion that we are self-made people. To Sabbath is to practise a reliance on the past, present and future activity of God. After all, we live by the imagination and breath of God, not by our own ingenuity and steam.

Sabbath assures us that we are not forgotten, that we are not overlooked. Sabbath gives us the gentle reminder that God has already been at work within our world and will continue to do so. Sabbath calls us away from the foolish idea that we need to attract our heavenly Father's attention, that we need to earn his love and favour. Sabbath is the voice of reason that tells us that there is more to life's existence than building empires. Sabbath calls to us in our insanity and says, 'You don't have to go, you know?' Sabbath is what summons us to abandon the Pool of Bethesda (the house of competition) and enter into expressing and celebrating the gift-life of God.

It's not just a challenge to certain religious leaders of His day; Jesus' Sabbath actions and words still speak to our own condition. To express love through Sabbath is to allow ourselves to be defined by God's work, and not simply our own.

There is one Sabbath however, beyond the Genesis narrative, where God doesn't seem to work.

It's the Saturday that follows the crucifixion.

Jesus dies on the Friday and remains that way until the Sunday. The God who never ceases to work appears to take the eternal rest.

But why the intermission? Why come back on the Sunday and not the morning of the actual Sabbath day? I really don't know why the wait exists, and I don't think we really have to explain it; all I do know is that for those who wept about the crucifixion, the Sabbath happens – God pauses history. This pause is important, like the creation story of Genesis; it makes the claim that His work is done. And then, on the first day of the week, He launches a New Creation, in the midst of the old.

Think about that for a moment. You cannot move from the Cross to the Resurrection without the Sabbath. In this sense then, the Sabbath functions in the same way as it always has – you have to accept that the work is done, and it was not by our efforts! At the cross **it is finished**, and the Sabbath focuses our call away from achievement and on to expressing what God has achieved. Sabbath once more reminds us that it wasn't our work that liberated us; it has only come through the interjection of God's power.

We are a New Creation – but it is God's hallmark that is stamped into the finished piece.

We do not work for our salvation, but as Paul tells us, we are to 'work *out* [our] own salvation...for it is God who works *in* you...'.[16] New creation life becomes an expression of God's work within us and not an attempt by us to earn some kind of status, whether that's *salvation* or *blessing* or *acknowledgement*, via our performance.

This truth should then massively alter the body of the church, especially those few streams that call for the *Insanity* work-out style of performance. Instead of being Christian alternatives of the world's rat-races, churches are free to become houses of rest. Or as Sarah Bessey puts it (in regards to women, but also equally applicable to all), '*We need our gathering together to be a place of detox from the world – its values, its entertainment, its priorities, its skittered fears, its focus on appearances and materialism and consumerism'.*[17]

Churches can be places where we don't need to jump and shout to inform God and the world of who we are, but communities that gather to receive and reflect God's definition of our identity.

Just to clarify; I'm not against work, I'm not against volunteering, or programmes, or 'church growth' per se. I am for learning, and growth, and development – but, is our activity defined and motivated by the fear of being a nobody, or is our momentum recognition that, in Christ, we already are somebodies; that our own sense of esteem, our sense of value, our sense of worth, don't rest in ourselves and our own achievements but in Jesus, in a reality that is unobtainable through our own efforts, yet freely available to us because of His? As Tim Keller reminds us,

> *'Our self-image rests in a love we cannot lose, and a beauty that does not dim.'*[18]

It takes love to practise Sabbath – to take time observing and acknowledging that we are loved by God, to such an extent that we can stop being consumed by our need to exhale life into our own personal vision of the world, and begin to inhale and exhale God's vision for/of His creation.

But it doesn't just stop there.

NO CONTEST

As I mentioned briefly in the chapter *Worship*, Sabbath plays an important part in forming our perspective of who God is. As this chapter has also tried to explore, Sabbath also forms our perspective of who we are. But it also calls us to reflect on who *they* are too.

As many commentators have pointed out, the commandment of Sabbath sits as a junction between the previous three commandments that deal with the nature of our relationship to God, and the following six that deal with the nature of our relationships with the rest of created life.

Sabbath sets the perspective on life.

Those who express love through the practice of Sabbath stop seeing life as a playing board; because of this they don't dishonour the generations that came before them – they don't belittle the progress that their ancestors did or didn't make. They aren't so engrossed with their own individualistic pursuits that they forget they are part of something more substantial than self. They don't need to steal, or lie, or murder in order to *gain* or *advance* or *build*. They will refuse to see people as toys for sex; they understand that every person has value, that everyone is someone – that no one exists solely for the pleasure of another. People who practise Sabbath have thrown away the competitive edge, they refuse to play comparisons, they have done away with the need to covet, they stop seeing someone else's *'grass as greener'*, they no longer live on *'the fad of the land'* diet that society serves them.[19]

To practise Sabbath is to break away from the regime of *achieve*, *accomplish*, *perform* and *possess*. To practise Sabbath is to reject the methods of Egypt. In turn, this prevents us from categorising our neighbours, using labels related to the production mechanism of existence, labels like 'cogs' or 'spanners'.

Our expression of love is nuanced by Sabbath, because we will never ever be truly capable of *'loving our neighbour'* as long as we continue to view the people around us as commodities, capital or competition.

For the Hebrew nation, Sabbath was never intended to just be *a* day – every seven years there were Sabbath years, when slaves were released and debts cleared – and every seventh Sabbath year, there came the Jubilee. The practice of Sabbath was more than a twenty-four hour period of rest, it was designed to permeate the whole fabric of social life, it was to define business ethic, it was to set limits to mankind's exploitation of nature, it was meant to be the ethos of an alternative culture.

As the story goes, however, it was never really realised. But in Christ, the one who offers us rest from our labour, that alternative is still on offer – if we'd be willing to accept it?

I've signed myself out from the space-race. Some may mark that as failure, but it's the proudest 'failure' I've made. You see, I tried it, and it nearly killed me. And if it weren't for the loving expression of those around me, whose friendship and support reminded me that I am more than a playing-piece in the game of life, I could have potentially lost myself for good.

I cannot say 'thank you' enough to those people.

To Paul – thanks buddy!

To my amazing better half Steph, thank-you for loving me. Thank you for giving me the words of God, words that I now leave for whoever is reading these pages – 'You don't have to go, you know?', or to rephrase that in a more familiar way for some:

'Be still, and know that I am God' – Psalm 46:10 (NKJV)

'Then Jesus said to them, "The Sabbath was made to meet the needs of people, and not people to meet the requirements of the Sabbath" ' – Mark 2:27 (NLT)

EXPRESSED THROUGH **PRAYER**

'In the silence of the heart God speaks'
Gonxha Agnes Bojaxhiu (Mother Teresa)[1]

GREEN WITH ENVY

When I was a boy, I enjoyed those sick days at home and having to stay off school. Don't get me wrong, I didn't enjoy being ill, and I did, honestly, enjoy school. But having the day off had its advantages – the main one being that I got watch *Sesame Street*.

It was the best show to watch as a child, in some ways even more educational than school, as it didn't just deal with the intellectual things, but also with the heart things. It talked about stereotypes, bullying, friendships and how to see the world[2]. They were powerful messages to convey into the life of a kid just like me, and to help the transmission of those messages was an amazing array of teachers – *The Cookie Monster* who, when looking back, was almost like some tragic Greek mythological character, endlessly consuming cookies, only to have them crumble to dust and fall out of his mouth; *Bert and Ernie*, who consistently showed what it meant to be great friends; *Mr Snuffleupagus*, the earless pachyderm on whose back I wanted to climb; *The Count*; *Oscar the Grouch*; *The Two-headed Monster* that used to put word sounds together; *Elmo* (Wow, that episode where *Elmo* learns to tie his shoelaces is legendary!). There was this mighty pantheon of personalities that I enjoyed watching and learning from – with the exception of *Big Bird*, I found him scary.

However, there was one occupant of 'The Street' that I loved most – *Kermit the Frog*[3]

In particular, it was those scenes where *Kermit* would find himself sitting on a wall accompanied by a child. While sitting there, they would share conversation together – the child would talk and *Kermit* would listen. The children would open up about all kinds of things, sharing their fears, their questions, their perceptions of the world – most of which probably just sounded like cute talk or gibberish to some adults – but to me, well, I shared some of those views and concerns. As they shared, *Kermit* would respond and nod his head, and then finally give his counsel. It wasn't that Kermit would wave some magic wand and remove their issues and fears, he didn't. But through *Kermit*, his creator Jim Henson offered a fresh perspective on seeing the world around them, and the world within them, and the discrepancies that often occurred between the two. And at the end of the conversation would come the embrace – he would always leave them with the knowledge that they were loved and cared for.

I'd watch those scenes with envy, wanting to be the child on the wall who got to talk to Kermit, who received a hug at the end of the conversation... I still do!

I long for communion.

I think we all do, don't we?

We crave to be understood, to converse, to be intimate in a way where no barriers exist.

I mention this because as we begin our look at love expressed through prayer, I am aware that a multitude of books already exist which are devoted to the subject – some great, some 'ok-ish' – but lots of them, all offering fresh perspectives about different kinds of prayer, how to 'keep going in our prayer life' and how to 'spice-it-up' when it begins to wane.

I'd encourage you to read widely and deeply from those books as they give valuable insight about the topic at hand, using a much larger and more substantial format than this chapter alone can offer. But, I need you to know that within this chapter I'm not attempting to do what they do.

This isn't a theological study into prayer. Neither is this an exploration of the nine types – no, five types – or is it eight types – of prayer that exist.

I just want to get to the *something* that underlies the heart of all of that – that prayer is ultimately about being with God; taking time out with Him to sit on the wall of life, to share ourselves with Him, and in turn to allow ourselves to be shaped and formed by the fresh perspectives and viewpoints of a heavenly Father who deeply longs for humanity to receive His embrace.

Sometimes however, it's our analysing of prayer that actually gets in the way of this.

METHOD, MADNESS, MAGIC

When we think/talk about prayer, the conversation often begins to revolve around methodology, form and structure – i.e. when to pray, how to pray, what words to use... how to start, how to end.

I'm certain that you and I, and anyone else reading this book, have our different methods at prayer; if we carried out a quick survey, I'm sure there would be a wide range of results.

Some of us would champion getting up in the morning and meeting the day with prayer. For others, we feel more comfortable praying last thing at night as it suits our night-owl personalities. While yet others grab some time with God while in the 'pod' of their vehicles on the way to and from work.

Some prefer to pace around the room talking in an audible voice (with occasional shouting), whereas others prefer to sit in silence and contemplate. Some feel they pray better when alone, while other individuals feel they come alive when prayer becomes corporate.

We might put our hands together and close our eyes, while some love to pray with their eyes open and have their hands free to embrace the warmness of their coffee cup. We may use prayer journals, or candles, or rub a rock, or even use a rosary. Some might use the words of old hymns, or the book of Psalms, or the common book of prayer, while others just prefer to be spontaneous. Some of us might still say amen at the end of our prayers (even when we are on our own), yet for others it's hard to distinguish where their prayer ends.

I suspect for most of us, our prayer-life might look like a meshing together of all of that, plus more besides.

Whatever our methods, it's important to note that they are just *methods* – they *are* just rhythms that help us to personally spend some time in the embrace of God.

In the gospel accounts of Matthew, Mark, Luke and John, we are given glimpses of Jesus' 'how', when it came to prayer.

He prayed both publicly and privately. He prayed out loud and quietly. He prayed in religious spaces and secular spaces (for those who prefer to cling to those divisions). He prayed on mountain tops and in deserts. He prayed standing up and sitting down. He prayed in the morning and at evening time – sometimes even through the night! He prayed with people, for people, for friends, for enemies, and for Himself. There are times when He prays looking 'up' to heaven, and a time when He falls, face down, on the ground. Jesus was able to pray while enjoying life, while being in the company of people, and He was still able to pray even while people crucified Him.

And yet when Jesus prayed, the impression you get is that this wasn't ritual – even if its form sometimes was – but relational.

For Jesus, it wasn't the *how, when* and *what* that was important, but the *with*. He wanted to spend time *with* the Father.

As I've said, you will have your methods, I have my methods – methods that have changed throughout the seasons of life, and will inevitably continue to change – but we can't afford to mistake our methods for the actual intended interaction that prayer is.

Our methods are purely containers that provide an environment for the chemical mix of divine and human to react.

Let me put it another way.

There are lots of ways I spend time with Steph – eating, watching a film, going for a walk, working together, doing chores around our home, phone calls, emails, Skype... but regardless of the vehicle, they are just *ways* that allow me to interact with her and enjoy her company. Yes, some might say that 'some of those are romantic, while others are mundane' – but that's beside the point – if the only time I spend relating to Steph is when the setting is romantic, then what sort of relationship is that? It's hardly sharing life together.

The problem is that we can sometimes place *our* method on a pedestal that it shouldn't occupy – we confuse our method with what prayer is, which in turn devolves prayer into something it isn't, and when we do this the inevitable happens:

We get shocked and defensive when we discover other people don't get up at five in the morning like we do – so we question their 'commitment', saying that those people can't really love God, at least not as much as *we* do.

Those who observe the 'silent ones' wonder if they're actually asleep – while those who listen to the 'shouters' wonder if they're simply making noise in an attempt to keep themselves awake.

We hear a liturgical/read style of prayer and question whether the person means it, or we judge the prayer as not being an expression of love because it, we assume, uses words that are borrowed – while at the same time we fail to appreciate that every word we use is borrowed in some sense, and that many people have been known to say a lot of things spontaneously which they didn't mean and which weren't really thought through.

We can become judgemental of people who don't seem to use the proper prayer language, or who don't have the correct posture – assuming that it's because of their immaturity. Of course, this too evolves because when our idea of prayer is based on etiquette, we begin to classify people as being 'good' or 'bad' at it, even ourselves. So, when we want prayer, we'll seek and ask those who meet our standard of fluency to pray for us – and when someone asks *us* to pray, we begin to feel this tremendous pressure to make sure we say the right things in the right ways – because it's got to sound impressive to be effective, hasn't it?

You see, when we think of prayer as a technique, then what we are really doing is making a statement that there is only one way in which interaction with God can take place.

And that's true!

But that interaction is not through a method, or a certain time of day, or a specific place or posture... it's a person – Jesus, God in flesh[4]. When we consider this, then we should begin to see that prayer is not about formalities, but relationship – and relationship is messy, non-uniform, and flexible. It 'fleshes' itself out everywhere, in different ways and in different places. There's really only one way to pray properly then – by actually doing it.

There's a further issue too, when we confuse prayer with method; when we adopt a mindset which believes that the only way our prayers will be heard and answered is if we do them in a certain way, at a certain time, in a specific location, by saying particular words... then really, what is the difference between saying a prayer, and say, casting a spell?

When our *method* becomes what prayer *is*, instead of our interaction with God, we risk moving from relationship to superstition, and superstition is not an expression of love.

'GA-GA'

Prior to giving us what we now know as *The Lord's Prayer*, Jesus said these words – *'When you pray, don't babble on and on as people of other religions do. They think their prayers are answered only by repeating their words again and again. Don't be like them, because your Father knows exactly what you need even before you ask him!'*[5].

After reading that, maybe those with particular methods that draw on the above text might be thinking, 'Aha, see, there is a right way to do it'. But that isn't the point of what Jesus is saying here. This verse, and the one before it, are not treatises against praying out loud, or about asking more than once. After all, Jesus prayed out loud[6] and he gave teaching about being persistent with our requests[7].

When Jesus is talking about this repetitive incantation of words – a repetition done in an *effort* to be heard – then He's tackling the mindset we've just been discussing. He's trying to straighten out this strange idea that it's only through some kind of prescriptive performance on our part that somehow enables us to invoke God's attention and blessing on our lives. Jesus' words startle us with the reality that God does not depend on our activity to initiate the conversation – the Father is already intimate – God's the one who's seeking us.

Jesus paints a picture of a God who is not aloof, a God who we don't need to shout and wave at in the hope of catching His attention, a God who doesn't keep Himself locked behind closed doors that can only be entered by knowing the right password, or by performing something like a spiritual version of the *Truffle Shuffle*[8].

Jesus tells us of a God who is close to us, who knows us – a God who is so present in our lives that He already knows what we need before we ask. And Jesus isn't sharing that last nugget of information with us just so that we can go away and shape another method that hinges itself on 'not asking' of God at all. Jesus exposes this truth in order to encourage us to pursue intimacy with our creator, in the knowledge that we don't have to jump through burning hoops before we can even begin to share our deepest worries and heart-felt concerns. God's omniscience (the posh word for 'all-knowing') is not an excuse to not seek communion with God (in some ways, that's abusive of His knowledge – if I didn't speak to Steph about something that I knew she was aware of, that would be labelled as 'avoidance', I think?). Knowing that God knows should inspire us to come as we are into a space that is secure and where pretence and performance are not required.

'*Our Father...*' is the picture Jesus wants us to grasp – the visual that Jesus wants us to hold at the forefront of our minds as we pray – not the picture of '*Our God*'. That's not to degrade God's divine status, or holiness – it's just that sometimes, maybe often, we use God's difference to reinforce our methodological approach. 'Father' shifts our focus point away from an 'up there', 'far beyond', 'someone who must be travelled to' personality to one who is *here, present, caring.*

I've learnt a lot from my kids. One of the things I've experienced is that my children didn't have to know *how* to communicate with me before they *could* commune with me. Neither of us, as parents, asked that of them when they emerged out of the womb – we just welcomed them to our environment and made them aware of our presence.

As parents, we'd just spend time with our children, and the conversation came without being forced. At first the language is simply 'Ga-Ga' and 'Gu-Gu', accompanied by other strange noises, cries, smells and random wiggles – none of which seem as sleek or sophisticated as we 'grown-up and experienced' adults are used to. But our children's undeveloped skills never once damaged the quality of our communion with them.

As they've grown and their experience has deepened, words have formed – along with recognition and use of body language – and so new layers within our relationships begin. They understand me more clearly (although, they often pretend not to) and I understand them (kind of!). But regardless of how refined they/we become in the use of speech and language, or art and music, it's still just an attempt to communicate our thoughts and feelings through some form/method, whether that's sounds or movements or pictures.

Now, please stay with me here.

God is Father.

He's so much bigger than us and so much more experienced and grown-up compared to us. In fact, His thoughts and ways are so higher than ours[9], that irrespective of how sophisticated or effective we feel our methods of communication have become, from His perspective they probably resemble the wiggles and 'Ga-Ga's' of a newborn infant.

But that's ok. God doesn't belittle us or command us to try harder, because the method isn't what prayer is – the form is secondary – it's all about the embrace. As a loving Father holding His child, He doesn't look down His nose at us because of our clumsy ways – He draws closer to us, cherishing every movement. He brings His face nearer to us, so we don't have to strive in our grasping. As a parent, He initiates – He bends down and listens, giving His undivided attention to our every sound. How can we not respond to such attention?[10]

In His expression of love towards us, God invites us to commune with Him – He calls us onto the wall with Him, to share and to talk and to listen. And in our expression of love back to Him, all we need to do is accept, nothing else. Prayer is not about us using some kind of performance to appease God in order to have an audience with Him for a few moments[11] – prayer is *us responding* to *God's gracious request* to be with Him.

I hope that releases some of us, because if we grasp that, we'll begin to see that *our* methods aren't what's important. Actually, to borrow some words from Brennan Manning:

> '*The most important thing that ever happens in*
> *prayer is letting ourselves be loved by God*'[12].

So don't get too worried about doing it right, because knowing what Jesus teaches has led me to the discovery that I can't get spending time with God wrong.

But even when we put *form* in its proper place, there is still another thing that tries to compete for the definition of prayer and dismantle it from being an expression of love.

CURIOSITY KILLED THE CAT...

I don't know but maybe, like me, you've got *those* stories about prayer. I'm going to share one of mine with you. However, as most stories go, they nearly always involve other people, and this one is no exception. So to keep identities confidential, we're going to call the other character in this story Bob.

Bob's a good name, it gives nothing away.

As any youth worker/leader will know, when you happen to live on the same estate as where you do youth work, your home runs the extreme possibility of becoming a drop-in centre. And so, at some point during our time in our little main road terrace, we had every one of the young people that we worked with turn up unannounced, all in different states and all for very different reasons.

Bob had been coming to our youth group for a short while and had begun to ask questions about this whole 'Jesus-thing'. Like most teenagers – and grown-ups – Bob was prone to emotional ups and downs, many of which we'd witnessed and experienced by this point. But we'd never seen Bob in anything like the state we discovered as we opened our door on this particular evening – he was an emotional wreck, wet, tears, shaking, pale, just not in his right mind. It took Steph and me a good quarter of an hour to persuade Bob to come in out of the cold and to have a seat. And even when that task was completed, it still took more time before Bob was in a calm enough state to talk.

Without going into any of the detail, there had been an accident at home while Bob's parents were out – a misjudgement that had resulted in the death of their household cat. In a storm of panic over what had happened – and a deep terror of the consequences that would surely follow once the parents returned – Bob had decided to bag the body, throw it down a nearby ditch and attempt to walk-off the emotions, while coming up with a cover story (something along the lines of 'the cat got out'). However, after walking for an hour, Bob realised that the clutches of guilt aren't easy things to shake off, and so in his helplessness, he had decided to come to us for help.

Now, you need to know that I'm an animal lover – to the great extent that I'll even aid in the evacuation of spiders and wasps from our home (spider-size dependent, of course). But I'm also human – I've done things I'm not proud of, things that have resulted in consequences that I didn't think could happen and that I didn't think through – even when they were obvious afterwards. So I didn't 'shop' Bob to animal welfare, as what Bob described was, I believe, an accident – but, I didn't just dismiss it either and label it as 'ok' or condone Bob's mistake. I just simply asked, 'How can we help?' – with the aim of helping Bob to begin making some better choices in the midst of this mess.

Bob decided that the first thing we should do was to go and get the cat. So we did.

Bob led me to the ditch, pointed out the bag's location, I climbed down to retrieve it, and then we began to make the journey back to our house with the cat cadaver in tow. As we walked, we talked, and Bob started to raise questions about God's love for him in the light of the current situation. I tried my best to assure Bob that there was no question of God's love for him. The thing is though, when you get into conversations like that, in such circumstances, then the inevitable question eventually shows up – 'If God still loves me, do you think He'll bring my cat back to life, do you think He can?'

How do you answer that, because you know where questions like that are going to end up? Seriously, how? This stuff should be written on some sort of pocket-sized survivors' guide entitled: 'Great question, Wrong moment'.

Before I could even begin to fuddle something together resembling an answer, I was suddenly reminded, verbatim almost, of everything I had taught in the youth meetings with regards to prayer. I was actually kind of surprised to find that Bob had been listening. Bob was pulling me out quote for quote, and with scripture backup! By the time we'd made it to my house the preach was just coming to an end, and without giving me even the slightest bit of space to manoeuvre out of the corner I'd been backed into, Bob threw the final KO punch – 'Will you pray for it, because you said God answers prayers, so you have to?'

I really had no defence, 'Ok?'

What was I thinking? I'm not sure. I wanted to say 'no', but my head was split in two. One side of me thought, 'This isn't impossible for God, so maybe He will. If He did raise the cat, that would be amazing – imagine the effect it would have on Bob's life, it would be a proper 'ta-da, God's real' moment. Imagine the testimony Bob would be able to tell friends and family... but... that would kind of mean having to explain *all of this* to the family!' Whereas the other half of me was thinking, 'It's a cat! A cat that's been dead for two hours! Is God really going to bother with this, with all the other "big" stuff going on in the world? And then there was that 'runny nose' I had the other week, and God did nothing about that...'

But I said I would, so I did.

So there I was, kneeling in the back yard of our terrace, getting soaked by the drizzling rain, laying my hands on the body of a dead cat, praying for God to breathe life back into its corpse.

...OR DID IT?

We'll come back to that particular cat, but first a question:

Have you ever wondered *why* you pray?

That's not a trick question either.

One answer that praying people give to that question is, 'Prayer changes things', but does it? If it does, and we believe that, then is that the *only* motive for our prayer? If prayer doesn't change things, would we still pray? And if the answer is both 'yes' and 'no', or better phrased 'maybe', then where does that leave us?

Now please stay with me here, because we'll go round this the long way.

There's a famous thought experiment in physics called *Schrödinger's Cat*. You may have heard of it, you may have not. The idea in theory, but for obvious reasons not in practice, is to take a live cat and seal it inside a box, along with a radioactive substance and a vial of poisonous gas. Also in the box is a Geiger counter, which will measure the presence of nuclear decay within the sealed box. If/when the counter detects nuclear decay (radioactivity), it will then trigger a switch that will break the vial, releasing the poison, and killing the cat.

Before your mind gets distracted – no, this isn't what happened to Bob's cat!

So, after setting up the experiment (in our minds, remember), the question posed is, 'After one hour has passed, is the cat dead or alive?'

Of course, the easy way to discover the answer is to open the box and to take a peak. But the most important rule of the experiment is that we *cannot open* the box at the end of the hour (and no, you can't shake it either, or throw something at it – and yes, it's a naturally silent cat that we put in there in the first place). This may seem a strange way of doing things, but the idea behind the thought experiment is not whether *we observe* a dead or live cat at the end of one hour, but what is the state of the cat while we *cannot* observe it?

Because we can't open the box, we can't actually give a proper answer, so our answer becomes reliant on probability – the radioactive material may have had one of its atoms decay in that one-hour window, it may not, and that determines everything else. We could, potentially, have one dead cat in a box, or one cat that is extremely disgruntled for having been sealed in there for an hour.

As we can't look in or shake the box, or poke it with a stick, the only conclusions we are left with are 'yes' *and* 'no' – again, more accurately described as 'maybe'. In the 'laws' of probability the cat has entered into what is known as *superposition*; it no longer occupies a single state, but has the possibility of two – after one hour it's both dead, and alive.

Of course, that sounds bonkers – as far as we're concerned, there is only one reality – the cat is either dead *or* alive – but you can never be *certain* of that without opening the box up and looking (or by picking it up and giving it a shake), and that *uncertainty* is the whole reason for this brain-teaser.

You may remember that Werner Heisenberg quote at the beginning of the chapter on *Learning*, about nature being affected/exposed by our observations. That quote, and this strange thought experiment, all developed out of the weird things that were being (and still are being) discovered through quantum mechanics – the exploration of the workings and rules that govern the atoms and particles that make up everything around us.

One of the laws theorised regarded the movements and whereabouts of the smaller things that make up atoms, and the smaller things that interacted with them – things like electrons and quarks and photons and gluons. What was proposed was that these particles didn't exactly exist in one place, at one time (or one state). They could be anywhere and everywhere all at once – they exist in probability waves, multiple possibilities, *superposition* – they exist in *maybes*.

Which is odd, if you think about it for a moment.

Because you're made up of substances – substances formed by mixtures of chemical elements – elements that are formed by different interacting clumps of atoms – atoms that are energy-driven relationships of all this smaller stuff, like electrons and quarks. And what's being said here, as an example, is that the electrons which are a key part of the building blocks of what makes your body, don't exist in one place like your body does – they're everywhere, unlike you.

Quantum physics proposes that these electrons exist in a constant state of possibility – here and there – *until* we choose to 'ask' about their movements – until we choose to interrogate them about their whereabouts – until we choose to 'observe' what they are doing or where they are going, and then, and only then, do these possibilities collapse into a single reality. Apparently, opening the box on nature causes it to *be*.

I know, it sounds crazy – that reality exists as it does because it is being observed, that nature behaves like it does because our (or something/one else's) curiosity causes it to give an answer.

This crazy idea of reality is why one of the physicists involved in these explorations, a man named Erwin Schrödinger, came up with the cat-in-a-box thought experiment as an attempt to demonstrate how ludicrous this seems. Does nature behave like *Schrödinger's cat* – which, while it isn't being 'observed', fluctuates between possibilities, but once the box is opened causes those probabilities to collapse into *a* reality? If so, that leaves us with a further question: Was it really the poison, or was it *our* curiosity that killed the cat? Who's really to blame?

So why the science illustration?

Please don't misunderstand my reasons; I am not trying to use science to prove the power of prayer; I am *not* saying that my prayer somehow observes a better reality and forces it to exist. I wouldn't even think of going there.

I'm simply using the cat in a box as a metaphor for our own prayers – that maybe for some of us, in our prayer life, we sometimes act like *we* carry the responsibility for the results of what we'll discover when we open the box. That whatever happens, rests solely with us and our prayers, that it's the quality of our interaction that defines the outcomes.

Or to phrase that another way, because you might have had it said to you this way: 'It didn't happen because you didn't believe enough'.

Really?

Did my Mum and Dad die because I didn't believe enough? Did Steph experience a miscarriage because, maybe collectively, we just didn't have enough 'juice' to push the gauge on the faith-o-meter out of the red zone of doubt? What about our children? One of them is on the autistic spectrum and the other is profoundly deaf in one ear. Where does that responsibility lie, with us as parents, or with them?

And if we're taking responsibility for everything that comes out of the box, then what about the state of the world? Are we, the 'believers', responsible for all those unobserved realities – realities filled with laughter instead of tears, peace instead of war, love instead of abuse – never coming to pass?

What about Bob's cat? Because, after five minutes of what I thought was some pretty good praying, this particular cat certainly didn't occupy a state of superposition; it was still, very much, dead. Am I to blame?

It's right that we pray about the things that pull on our hearts – these things matter to us, so it's natural that they will come up in our conversations with the One who knows our needs. And even the things that are not natural to us, by praying for them, they can become concerns of our hearts. But it's extremely dangerous when we begin to blame the quality or quantity of our prayer for the reality that comes spilling out of the box of life.

Yes, there are those (maybe yourself) who would put it down to a lack of faith – but there are times when I have given everything I have to seeking and asking, and I'm certain there will be many who read this who have too. It's not formulaic like that! And when we give clichéd answers like 'You didn't believe enough', all we do is fill people up with condemnation, guilt and fear (we're also indirectly causing them to put more trust in their efforts and methods too) – which is hardly the prayer life Jesus desires and motivates us to pursue.

I have my fair share of disappointments and frustrations when it comes to 'unsuccessful' prayer. I don't know why my father died, despite seeing him miraculously pull through a coma on a high-dependency ward weeks before. I have no idea why our own family, as well as families around us, have had to endure some really horrible circumstances. I cannot explain how a praying man ends up having a breakdown.

I don't know. I ask...

...sometimes a little...

...sometimes a lot.

I'm all for faith. I'm a firm believer that prayer does change things, but I am also acutely aware that when reality does reveal itself (and it only ever reveals itself through one reality at a time, certainly not through 'maybes'), it doesn't always resemble my requests; that after an hour I come to the box to discover that it contains things unhoped for. Which of course raises the question, does prayer actually *do* anything?

In the case of Bob's cat, we could conclude that prayer did nothing because the results Bob and I were seeking didn't manifest themselves (or maybe some would rephrase that as '*I* did nothing', as God is able, so the fault must lie with me?). Of course, on the flip side, if the cat had come back to life, then the critics of prayer would still say that prayer didn't do this. But, is such thinking right – is that what prayer is *all* about, is the end goal results?

REALITY CHEQUE

To return again to the question that prompted all this: Is that *why* we pray, and what happens to our praying when what we want isn't found inside the box? Do we just stop the conversation?

We've already considered the snare that method can be in our expression of love through prayer, especially when we mistake our methods as being prayer. Well, *results* are another thing that we often confuse prayer with. In fact, it can often be the results we seek that define, or cause us to refine, our methods.

And when both *method* and *results* join forces in our thinking, then we really are back to the basics of magic – that through some accurately articulated procedure we can invoke a supernatural power to do our bidding. If these two things begin to define what prayer is for us, then really, what makes God all that different from a genie – someone we summon to grant our wishes through rubbing His lamp the right way? Or a lawyer – who steps in to clear away our indiscretions once we've paid him for services rendered? Or a pool of water – which, once we act in the appropriate way and with the right consistency, will then produce the reality we so desire to observe?

We're right back to where we began – trying to get the machine to accept our currency – instead this time we're using prayer (and our fluency with it) as the means to pay God off, hoping that He will then cash the cheque on our desired reality. Instead of love, we're back to control.

> *'...I ask myself whether I have been*
> *primarily pursuing the results of my prayer*
> *rather than companionship with God'*[13]

First and foremost, prayer is conversation with the Father. It's a prime conduit for knowing Him – exploring who He is and becoming more aware of His faithful and consistent presence within our lives.

Sadly, and I'm speaking from my personal prayer experiences here, our prayers can sometimes feel like all we're really doing is rummaging around in our Father's pockets, seeing what He's brought home for us, instead of us actually growing familiar with Him – we want what He has, or what He can do, but we seldom welcome *who* He is. Alternatively, when we're not seeking something in particular, then the creator can still be of *use* to *us* as a divine agony aunt, someone to offload our concerns onto. But then, when we have nothing to hunt for, or no problems to talk about, the conversations stop – we don't show at all.

The issue is that *does* – we feel that God has to *do* something for us, and that prayer is the means of making this happen.

I'm not immune to this. There have been plenty of times when I've seen God as someone whose role is simply to provide for me and make me feel better. So I'm speaking to myself here within this chapter, as I too can turn up to pray, shopping list in hand, sometimes even with well-rehearsed words in my head, clinging to the illusion that the results depend on my performance – that if I do well enough, then God will hand me what I want on a silver platter (which reminds me of something that I said in the eleventh endnote of this chapter, just in case you missed it).

But this isn't love – relationships that place priority on *utility* over *unity* are not companionships, they're simply associations. Really, this is fairly narcissistic, using God as a means of personal gratification, which in turn means that we'll measure how *useful* prayer is by looking at how it best facilitates ourselves and our lives.

What about God?

Love expressed, as I discussed in an earlier chapter, seeks to know the object of its love. Like most other love-orientated conversations, prayer is time spent looking at and discovering who the other is.

Yes, God is a *Wonderful Counsellor*, so this in turn flavours the contents of my prayers – I share openly and honestly about how I feel, knowing that He listens, that He's patient, that He keeps things confidential, that He gives guidance and helps me to turn the problems over in order to see them for what they really are.

Yes, God is the *Everlasting Father*. Again, hinting back to what was said earlier, He cradles us in His arms, showing us unrelenting affection. Knowing that His provision and care and love are unconditional and faithful, means I can approach Him with confidence, I am assured that I am wanted and valued.

But God is also *Mighty God*, a Holy (Holy, Holy, Holy) God. The Creator, the inventor, the mind behind the whole of the cosmos (and whatever lies beyond that). He is the King of kings, the Lord of lords. The Word. The Light. The Source. The Way, the Truth and the Life. He is the God who not only forms us in our conception, but who was also willing to come and lay down His life, and raise it again, in order that we could share eternity with Him.

When I realise that, I am humbled. Once more we need to see that it's an act of His grace, not our presentation, that He invites us at all into His presence. Yet He does so. Lovingly, He bids us to come. Through Grace, God makes Himself known to us and invites us to know Him, the ancient author of life.

God is Great. God is Greater. God is Greatest.

We might not see these things straight away as we initially respond to the graceful invitation He gives us to pray, but surely, as we spend time with Him, looking at Him, exploring Him, these things will eventually start to become apparent to us. And once they do – to echo the meaning of some of Tom Wright's words – then the epiphany experience of knowing a God who is larger than, or different to, our ideas and expectations should lead us to a place where we need to respond accordingly[14].

If the greatness of *who* God is doesn't affect, or permeate itself into our prayer life, then maybe we *are* doing prayer wrongly – and that's nothing to do with our methods, or a measure of results – but our receptivity to Him and His purposes.

Prayer isn't about results. The purpose of prayer is relationship; enjoying and receiving God's embrace, but also gaining His vantage point and acknowledging His will.

What does prayer really *do*? It exposes us to the reality of the divine, a reality we are called to explore and to express.

What if the thing that God wants us to receive most in our conversations with Him is not some alternate reality, but an assurance of a divine presence within, and a divine perspective on, our current reality – a presence and perspective that will ultimately change our response to our circumstances and lead us to be responsible within those circumstances? So prayer doesn't just become some 'spiritual exercise' in order to exert our authority over the external world, it becomes a spiritually-physical relationship with a greater authority that brings transformation internally, leading to responsibility externally.

Am I allowed to suggest that, without being labelled a heretic or a 'doubting Thomas'?

Yes, I believe in prayer. Yes, when I encounter problems or finally realise the problems that inflict our world, I bring them to God, seeking resolution. I pray because I want things to change, and I believe God is able.

So pray for change, and expect it – but shouldn't we equally expect it, and allow it, within ourselves? As Richard Foster reminds us:

'To pray is to change. Prayer is the central avenue God uses to transform us. If we are unwilling to change, we will abandon prayer as a noticeable characteristic of our lives'[15]

Some might say that my praying for Bob's dead cat was ineffective, I choose to differ. While praying, I kept getting this niggling, irritating voice come to me – I don't mean an audible voice, but a poke at my conscience, one that I couldn't ignore.

So at the end of my and Bob's prayer time, I turned to Bob and said, 'God's not going to do this. Not because He can't, but because He won't. You see, both you and I don't want God to raise a dead cat – we want Him to get you off the hook. But He wants you to go home and take responsibility for your actions'.

Which, after very little thought, we both decided was the best means of beginning to put this whole mess right.

LET *YOUR* KINGDOM COME

I'm writing this passage with mere weeks to go until Christmas. So forgive me here if you're currently reading this mid-summer. I must admit, I am a sucker for some of the commercial aspects of the holiday season. I love the carols and songs, I appreciate the colour and vibrancy that decorations and lights bring to a usually dark time of year. I physically struggle to resist the invitation to have a mince pie – or two – and I really do enjoy watching the movies with my family – one of our favourites being *Elf*.

I don't want to give any spoilers away here, but one of the main characters of the film *Elf*, is Santa Claus. Santa's a personality most of us are used to in the west – a hearty man whose mission is to make sure every boy and girl receives a gift at Christmas time. However, his generosity does vary depending on whether they've been naughty or nice. In the film *Elf*, things have become increasingly difficult for Santa to do his job, as the population of the world at large has ceased to believe in his existence. Without this belief, Santa's magic and power have become weaker and weaker, eventually culminating in the crash-landing of his sleigh within Central Park, New York, on Christmas Eve. Without the people's faith in his agenda, Santa's mission is doomed to failure.

Of course, God's not Santa – although I do think that the confusion about the whole 'naughty and nice' thing isn't the only character trait of *Old St Nick* that we've also misidentified as belonging to the God whom Jesus reveals to us.

Firstly, God is not working to bring about the individually desired 'wish lists' of the seven billion people who currently live on planet earth. He's working within the vision of His own agenda. You see, God has dreams too. God sees, more than we do, the discrepancies between the world orders that currently exist and the one that He desires to see. But God has already done something to turn this around; through the life of Jesus and through His resurrection, God has already birthed His world order within the present one. Through Jesus, the Kingdom of God has come. This Kingdom isn't some ethereal future realm that one day we hope we'll be whisked off to. The end goal of this Kingdom is not to divorce the physical from the spiritual, or to separate 'heavenly' things from 'earthly' things, but a mission that seeks to repair the marriage of the two. This Kingdom is present, now, working like yeast within a batch of dough, renovating and catalysing *what is* towards its climax of *what could/should be.*

The Kingdom of God = Heaven on Earth.

That's God's project, it always has been.

It's this dream that He longs for us to seek and ask for, but do we?

And here's where the crux of our confusion between God and Santa Claus comes in – God's powers are by no means boosted or incapacitated by our belief or disbelief in Him. Unlike Santa's mission in the movie *Elf*, our prayers don't kick-start this project, nor do they (to some extent) 'fuel' or advance this agenda, nor do they 'revive' and 'rescue' this project from mission failure. This work is already under way, it's already broken out and finding expression here and there, working and transforming our world into one that we all desire – a place without anguish, pain, suffering, injustice, and death. Our desires didn't start this activity, our continued desires don't prolong it – this is God's initiative, born through *His* love and faithfulness to His creation, an initiative centred upon the work of Jesus, not us.

Maybe some of us find that hard to believe – that the effectiveness of God's work doesn't depend on our praying; that without us and *our* tightly-squeezed-eyed, clenched-fisted, heel-tapping 'There's no place like home' style of 'Let your Kingdom come', that God's best laid plans will come to nothing. Really? Does that sound like an all-powerful deity?

Maybe some of us would quote that famous bit of scripture, where Jesus returns to His hometown of Nazareth ('...because of their unbelief, [Jesus] couldn't do any mighty miracles...'[16]) in order to add ourselves back into the equation. But we need to be careful here because if we follow that line of thinking, then what we're saying is that the power lies with the people and not with Jesus – that their unbelief was greater than His ability. Which isn't true. Jesus is the manifestation of the Kingdom of God, so when He goes home to Nazareth, God's Kingdom is present within their midst. It's not their lack of faith that incapacitates God's power – God's power stands amongst them, fleshed out, ready and willing to be grasped – actually it's Nazareth's refusal to see this that prevents them taking hold of it and seeing it expressed within their community. Nazareth preferred to see a carpenter, an offspring, a brother, and not God's love expressed. Their lack of faith didn't turn off God's power tap, it stopped them drinking from it.

Prayer is not what brings God's Kingdom in, rather, it's through prayer that God longs to open our eyes to His activity within our present reality. Prayer is where God mercifully awakens within us the desire to ask and to seek His commonwealth, and where He gracefully invites us and equips us to get involved with the task of fleshing out His manifesto. Our conversations with the creator are what ultimately lead us to be responsible within this creation in accordance to the agenda He has in mind.

To keep with the Christmas metaphor, please don't mistake me for the *Grinch* who's come to steal away the spirit of prayer, just like that green-furred character does with the spirit of Christmas. Some may think I'm saying that we shouldn't pray, that there's nothing gained through praying, but nothing could be further from the truth. So to be perfectly clear, I'm *not* saying you shouldn't pray for God's Kingdom to come, of course you should. But the *come* in that sentence is not about its *arrival* or trying to procure its *continuance* – to say *come*, is to ask for it to find expression through our lives.

'*Let your Kingdom come*' is what Jesus calls us to pray[17]. This could easily be read as a plea for God *to come and do* something – a claim that also says at the same time that He isn't already doing something – or maybe even perceived as a cry of '*Beam me up Scotty*', if our understanding of the Kingdom is of some other-worldly existence. However, if God's Kingdom really is at hand – touchable, available to grasp, pre-existent of our request – then wouldn't this be better understood as an offering-up from someone who is ready to surrender their will in exchange for God's?

To pray is to change. To pray is to be overwhelmed by the greatness of our God, a God whose Kingdom has already come amongst us. And to love God, and to love others through prayer, is to perceive and to subscribe to that Kingdom's activity.

SEEKER

In chapter eleven of Luke's gospel we're told that one day, after watching Jesus in prayer, one of His disciples asked, 'Lord, teach us to pray, just as John taught his disciples'[18].

Something strikes me about this – and I admit that it wouldn't have been obvious to the disciples. It's something that we can only see because of the hindsight we bring to this story. We know something about Jesus that the disciples still haven't quite figured at this point, although they eventually will – we know that Jesus is God in Flesh. And isn't prayer about spending time with God? Walking with Him, conversing with Him, learning from Him, participating in His Kingdom? So, haven't they already been praying?

Gracefully, Jesus indulges the question – He's not offended – and He gives them the model that we now know as 'The Lord's prayer'. He then goes on to encourage them to keep on asking, keep on seeking, keep on knocking, and finally concludes with the promise that God is a good Father, who gives good gifts and will give the Holy Spirit to any and all who ask.

But, did you notice that the disciple's question about prayer focuses on the *how*? They want to know *methods*. They want Jesus to teach them His form of prayer, just like John taught his disciples. Whoever asked is comparing praying techniques with someone else's – Jesus possibly has a technique that will gain them some advantage towards getting better results than the technique John had.

I mention this in closing because it will sum up what this chapter's been all about. First however, a quick reminder that the intent of this chapter wasn't to give an exhaustive treatment of the subject of prayer, but an attempt to demonstrate the expression of Love that it should be. So please, go and read some of those other books that discuss prayer in more length. But before you do, a question: Why are you reading those books, what is it you're trying to discover, what 'secret' are you trying to uncover? Could you wanting to read those books be just another version of the disciple's question, a search for better alternative methods?

I'll be honest with you. I read those books for the wrong reasons as well – often, I'm too busy seeking hints and tips on how to improve and tweak my methods in order to get better results, instead of actually seeking and subscribing to the manifest activity of God that's right in front of my face.

'Our Father in heaven,

Hallowed be Your name.

Your kingdom come.

Your will be done

On earth as it is in heaven.'

Matthew 6:9-10 (NKJV)

EXPRESSED THROUGH **HUMILITY**

'Many that live deserve death. And some that die
deserve life. Can you give it to them? Then do
not be too eager to deal out death in Judgement.
For even the very wise cannot see all ends'
Gandalf (J.R.R. Tolkien)[1]

DON'T FEED THE SCUM!

'Later, as Jesus left the town, he saw a tax collector
named Levi sitting at his tax collector's booth. "Follow
me and be my disciple," Jesus said to him. So Levi got
up, left everything, and followed him.

Later, Levi held a banquet in his home with Jesus as
the guest of honor. Many of Levi's fellow tax collectors
and other guests also ate with them. But the Pharisees
and their teachers of religious law complained bitterly
to Jesus' disciples, "Why do you eat and drink with such
scum?"

Jesus answered them, "Healthy people don't need
a doctor—sick people do. I have come to call not those
who think they are righteous, but those who know they
are sinners and need to repent." '[2]

Table manners, unfortunately, have often been cause to judge how refined somebody is. I've lost track of all the rules some of my school teachers attempted to instil in me about the 'art' of eating. Some of those rules seem like common sense, like it's rude to eat with the contents of your mouth on display and it's not sophisticated to burp at the table (although, if I remember my history lessons correctly, it wasn't that long ago that this was considered a compliment within the houses of the ruling classes – it was an insult to not say thank you by belching your satisfaction). Some of the other rules, however, weren't that obvious, and still aren't. For instance: Why can't I eat my dessert with a soup spoon, why do I need a different shape to scoop up custard? Why is it rude to rest your elbows on the table? What's with the strict ruling on which hand should hold what – wouldn't it be more antisocial if my food was accidentally flicked in the direction of someone else's plate while struggling to cut it with the 'correct' hand? And really, who set the boundaries on how your cutlery should be laid to rest on the plate when you've finished eating?

As I said, for some, our ability to keep these 'laws' displays our ranking – those who fail are obviously of lower class. For some, our table manners, like how we pronounce the letter *H*, betray our standards, our potential and our origins.

Personally, I think that's pompous.

However, how we eat does say something about us – it does display something of our personalities and our preferences. Take my children and a meal of sausages, mash and green beans for example:-

Our eldest son normally goes straight in for the best. Within seconds of starting his course the sausages will have disappeared, leaving him to then casually graze through the mashed potato trying to postpone the inevitable. Unfortunately though (from his perspective) he's not leaving the table until he's eaten his vegetables – which, by the time he gets to them, have usually gone cold, making the whole experience more unpleasant and reinforcing his idea of why greens are 'yuk' and should be kept to last.

Our youngest, on the other hand, is much more of a tactician. He loves his sausages as much as his older brother does, but for him that means they're something to work towards. So he'll generally eliminate the enemy (the veg') first, interspersed with the occasional forkful of mashed potato. And if his quest seems too great a challenge, he'll motivate his endurance with a small cut from one of his sausages, reminding himself of the 'joy that lies before him'. More often than not, he'll clear away the debris, leaving himself with one whole sausage to relish.

Their eating habits really do reflect their characters.

Jesus had eating habits too, habits that perfectly reflected His nature. However, some people didn't like how Jesus ate. Not everyone was happy with the standards on display and questioned Jesus' origins because of them. And it wasn't that Jesus refused to eat his vegetables, or that he drank the wrong wine to accompany the meat. The problem usually revolved around the issue of who Jesus chose to eat with.

Jesus ate with 'scum' (at least that's the word my version of the New Living Translation uses).

'Sinners and Tax collectors' is what is usually found in most translations of this passage. It's important to see that the terms function as labels, identity markers for people who aren't like those doing the describing. These words operate as tags to depict what *you are*, and what *we are not*. Words of this kind help certain groups or individuals to enforce distance and distinction from the others around them. They not only highlight who *they* are, but when a certain tone is used, they also raise their users up to loftier, elitist heights.

Sinners is a word that could be read in many ways depending on the century in which it was read. At the time of Jesus, however, it was generally a designation of those who were barred from worshipping at the Temple. Maybe they were ill (leprosy, haemorrhaging etc.) or they just didn't meet the Levitical standards in some other way. Maybe they were prostitutes or pagans/pagan sympathisers. Either way, these were the people who were seen as unclean, exempt from the blessings of the faith – for them the Temple was closed. Entering into a relationship with their creator would be impossible for them until they were cleansed, and their only available options for this were the unofficial spaces like the pool of Bethesda.

Interestingly, tax collectors got their own special grouping away from ordinary sinners. People like Levi (also known as Matthew) were especially disliked because of the job they were doing on behalf of the Romans who occupied the land of Israel. Tax collectors were taking money from their own oppressed people and giving it to the foreigner-occupation, monies which would continue to finance their military regime and governance. As such, tax collectors were seen as collaborators with the Romans, traitors of their own national identity and cause, back-stabbers, cheats, filth... scum.

Within the pages that follow I'm going to stick to using the word scum – I like the meaning it carries, although, of course, I don't agree with its use in this story. But the word scum really helps us to understand the disgust and disdain that these 'elite few' felt when they witnessed Jesus' table manners.

Imagine how you feel when you're exposed to the half-chewed saliva-saturated contents of someone's mouth as they eat – for these observers, this was worse than that.

They loathed these people, and they weren't too keen that Jesus was happy to sit around a table with them, sharing food and conversation, either. Which is what prompts them to ask Jesus' followers, *'Why do you eat and drink with such scum?'*

Scum!

How would you feel if you were described as scum? What comes to your mind when you hear that word? And please, be honest.

For me, scum's that stuff that forms across ponds and deprives it of oxygen; scum's the surface algae that chokes what little life there is out of the rest of the ecosystem and prevents the sunlight from reaching the depths. It's a parasitic viral contaminant – it's *the* problem that causes all the other problems and needs to be eliminated.

Scum's also a good term to describe what I find all over my car windscreen when I leave for work in the morning. It's been scattered there, overnight, by the birds that roost in the tree that I park my car under. Despite the nice bright purple colour that it occasionally exhibits (due to the local blackberry bushes) it still makes my nicely-washed car filthy – it's unclean and needs to be washed away.

Scum is that horrible mess that you occasionally step into when you're walking down the street – you know what I mean – you almost have to perform some kind of lopsided *Michael Jackson Moonwalk* in an attempt to dislodge it off the bottom of your shoe.

Scum – they use this word about *certain* people who are not like them.

We know what they're saying. Maybe we've even used it ourselves when describing somebody. They might not be using a swear word to say it, but some people can be socially unaccepting even while using socially acceptable language.

They're looking at the people Jesus is sharing company with and they see them as lesser than themselves. Maybe they don't even see them as people. To describe them as dust or dirt would be a half step in the right direction. Unlike dust, most people don't want to step in scum, we try our best to dodge it – and warn others to look out for it – as we travel down the road.

Scum is something you get rid of, you certainly don't feed it.

Jesus' manners have really thrown up large questions, in His critics' minds, about His reputation and origin, and in particular any claim He had of being the Messiah, the One who would bring in the Kingdom of God:

For some of the observers the Messiah would be a perfect, law-keeping man, a person who would honour the articles of the faith and the traditions of the Torah (as they understood them). For these people, God's Kingdom would come only when the whole of Israel would keep the Law perfectly – even if they only managed it for one day. So why, if Jesus is *the One*, would He be eating and drinking with those who fail to, or are unable to, keep those rules?

For others, God's Messiah would be a warrior king like King David or the Maccabees, someone who would come and lead an army to rid their homeland of the foreign pollutant. He would be the bringer of a military revolution – a tidal wave of terror towards their enemies, but a tsunami of triumph for those he was allied with. So why, if Jesus is *the One*, is He spending time celebrating with the very tax collectors who help finance the enemy's military regime? Why has He called one of them to learn from Him and be His disciple?

'Is this how a Messiah eats?'

Their question to Jesus' disciples could really be rephrased this way – "If Jesus really is the Messiah, then shouldn't He be eating with us, aren't we the beneficiaries of the new world order, the law-keepers, the nationalists, those who have been working to bring about God's Kingdom ? Why eat with the defecation of a corrupted society?"

This is deeper than eating habits. This is an issue about identities; who *we* are, who *they* are and who Jesus is. And sadly, whenever the question of 'who Jesus is' gets raised, it occasionally descends into a completely different question of 'Who is Jesus *for*?'

Jesus' answer, along with His eating routine, is a challenge to these people. He presents them with an alternative view of what the heart of the Kingdom is all about. Jesus sees His mission like a doctor's – He must spend time with the unwell if they're to be healthy. The Kingdom has come to restore, renovate and resurrect, not to restrict, repel or remove. Its agenda is to seek and to save those that are lost, not to further separate the lost from the found.

Jesus' eating habits open the Kingdom up to people that others think it should be closed permanently to – the scum.

And Jesus' eating habits haven't changed!

Some would be happy if the Kingdom's aim was to continue to exclude those who they feel are unworthy, those who deserve death, who contribute nothing to the cause. But Jesus – God in flesh, the one who sees all ends – hasn't come to deal out death in judgement. He has come to bring life to all who recognise their need for it. Really, it's those who fail to recognise this need, those who disregard Jesus' invitation, those who would rather think of others as scum and who think their own achievements and self-righteousness qualify them – they will be the ones who miss out.

Or as Jesus said elsewhere in His famous manifesto of the Kingdom:

> 'God blesses those who realize their
> need for him (the poor in spirit), for the
> Kingdom of Heaven is given to them.'[3]

Which reminds me of some of the stories Jesus told, making the same point as His response to the critics of His eating etiquette: the story of the *Prodigal Son* (thinking especially of the character portrayed by the older brother) and the *Story of the Great Feast* (thinking of those who refused the invitation, too preoccupied with their *own* agendas)[4]. Self-righteous pride keeps them all away from the party, not because they didn't get an invite, but because they don't think the invite's applicable to them and worthy of their response.

Humility really starts with a question – do we recognise *our need* for God?

CARRIED

Some of us don't think we *need* Jesus – and I'm talking to the Christians here! We want His Kingdom, we want Him around, but we think it's our works, talents, gifts and credentials that qualify us for it – 'we've earned it', we feel. Maybe some of us even think that the Kingdom needs us and what we have to bring. We come to God, not offering our lives, but our portfolios. We want Jesus to *need* us[5].

In this way, we sort of mistake Jesus for a divine version of Lord Alan Sugar and confuse discipleship with the TV show *The Apprentice* – we think it's about us demonstrating to Him what we have to offer, how profitable it would be to have us on board, how we would benefit His agenda.

I don't know if you've ever watched the TV show, but I tell you, when it gets to the elimination time, when one of the hopefuls has to go, it turns nasty – really nasty! The contestants usually turn on each other, pointing out every flaw and failing in the others who sit with them – it's basically about highlighting how unworthy *they* are, and how worthy *I* am. And a lot of this unworthy slander often boils down to the PH test of 'who put themselves into the task' and 'who was being carried by everyone else's hard work'. It then becomes a matter of defending your honour, showing that you're not the deadweight, you can carry yourself and others. The contestants' postures change when this happens. Just a moment before they were all sitting relaxed, elbows resting on the boardroom table (terrible manners!), and then, when the threat of hearing 'You're fired!' becomes a looming reality, they begin to sit upright, raising their shoulders, and their voices, pointing fingers, flinging accusations, boasting of their experience, all with the intention of knocking someone else down in order to stay up.

Of course if that doesn't work, then some eventually switch to the grovelling tactic, 'please, please, please Lord Sugar...' I have to mention the grovelling bit because – and I am jumping ahead of us a little here – this isn't humility either. The grovelling is still just an attempt to appeal to someone else's ego, while feigning the death of our own.

Similar to the contestants' motives on *The Apprentice*, maybe some of us want Jesus to hire us, not because we're interested in His agenda, but because we're looking for a big break for our own. We're after Jesus' investment into our story, when actually He's calling us into His.

The bottom line is that The Kingdom doesn't give job interviews, it gives invitations – and there's a huge difference between the two, a difference we should all be extremely grateful for. If Jesus was involved in *The Apprentice*, He wouldn't be sitting in Lord Sugar's chair, pointing fingers and measuring stats. Jesus would be sitting outside, in the waiting room, ready to graciously invite those who have been rejected.

For some of us, this is backwards – a bad business mindset. Like the religious leaders who criticized Jesus' meal times, we think He's choosing the wrong people. We don't get it, because some of us don't want to be carried, we want to earn it. We want our value and place to derive from our contribution. But there's no getting into this Kingdom except on the shoulders of Jesus.

Which reminds me, yet again, of another story Jesus told; a story of a lost sheep and a shepherd who goes in search for it, leaving ninety-nine others behind[6]. When the shepherd finds the lost sheep, he joyfully picks it up and throws it over his shoulders, carrying it home. Some of us, if we were that sheep, would have protested, *'We'll make our own way home thank you, just show us the way'*. We certainly wouldn't have shared the shepherd's joy. We wouldn't have even shared his mission. We'd want him to go looking for the best, the greatest, the healthiest and the brightest – but he seeks the lost; and being lost, or last, or least, is nothing to boast about. As Paul wrote:

> *'God saved you by His grace when you believed.*
> *And you can't take credit for this; it is a gift from*
> *God. Salvation is not a reward for the good things we*
> *have done, so none of us can boast about it'*[7]

He chooses us because He loves us, not because of our credentials. And often, it's those without the right credentials who are usually the best at seeing this and responding to it. While some of us complain, the others, like Levi, celebrate by throwing a party. Jesus has given them something better than alternatives like the pool of Bethesda, more beautiful than the Temple – God has brought His relationship directly to them. And in their perceived need of Him, they welcome Him, inviting Him home and sharing Him with others.

It's grace. None of us are worthy of the Kingdom, yet Jesus invites us to eat with Him.

This is great news for some of us... terrible news for others. It takes humility to receive this love expressed to us, to admit our need for it, to allow ourselves to be carried. And it also requires humility to express this love to others.

TAPEINOS

Humility is central to the expression of love. In fact, I have to ask, is it even possible to love without it?

Without humility, can we really serve one another? Would we ever show mercy? Could we worship in truth and pray 'Let your Kingdom come'? Learning would be impossible without it, and in the absence of humility would we ever really Sabbath and allow others to Sabbath, or would our world just continue stumbling forward on some ego-trip competition?

The Greek word for humility is *tapeinos*. It means to 'lay low'. In other words, not to *raise yourself* up, especially in comparison to others. It's the opposite of what you see demonstrated around *The Apprentice* boardroom table.

It's about not climbing over others and thinking of ourselves as superior.

Maybe there are people we see as scum, and for all sorts of reasons. Maybe some of those reasons we feel are substantiated through our own preferences, whether political, social, religious or moral. Maybe for some it does, sadly, purely boil down to manners. We're certainly not immune to the attitudes that inflicted the critics of Jesus' social life. Our present time is still full of labels – labels intended to be used to 'put others down' and 'raise ourselves up' over them. Names and words which, when used with particular tones, become a means of dehumanising some, while placing divine-like (or divine-*liked*) status on others.

But to practise humility is to stop this human branding, to stop seeing some as the 'nectar of the gods', and others as merely the dregs.

All human life has value because it's valuable to Him.

At the same time, to practise humility is not to see ourselves as scum either. Rather than acknowledge value where we would find someone repulsive, we can sometimes take the easy option and degrade all human life to a base level of being worthless, including ourselves. When practised this way, humility becomes characterised by self-loathing and becomes self-destructive.

We need to be careful to strike the right balance.

To be humble is to be empty of our own personal boasts and our own personal prejudices. It's to have a real understanding of who we are, to comprehend that our salvation, and everything that flows with that – peace, security, forgiveness, joy, inheritance – is solely a gift of God's grace.

None of us are worthy. Yet none of us are worthless. Someone has paid a high price for all of us[8].

If we understand this, then this will also define our expression.

To love though humility is to empty ourselves of self-promotion via our self-righteousness, but at the same time it's not to be empty per se – it's to be full of acknowledgement.

Let me put it another way.

HOLES DON'T EXIST

There's a special group of words we use in the English language, called *privatives*.

You'll use them all the time, trust me.

A perfect example of one of these special words would be the word *hole*. We say things like, 'I have a *hole* in my sock', or 'There's a *hole* in my bucket' – now think about that for a minute, think about what it is we're actually saying. Is there actually *a* hole in your bucket? This may come as something of a surprise, but holes don't exist. You can't go to a shop and buy a packet of ten holes; no one sells holes, and if anyone ever turns up on your doorstep offering a special today-only discount on some, turn them away! So how do you happen to have one in your sock or your bucket? When we use the word *hole* we're not describing the presence of something, but the *absence* of something. In the context of socks, we're not describing the existence of a hole, but the non-existence of the material. I suppose other examples could be *cold* (describing the absence of heat), *dark* (describing the absence of light), or *death* (describing the absence of life)[9].

Humility is not a privative. It's not the absence of self, but the presence of an acknowledgement of another.

It's not about us becoming non-existent, hollow and void. Our self, our character, doesn't disappear; it just re-orients itself about someone else. We are to be empty of personal boasts, but in the light of His grace towards us, we should in turn be full of His praise.

Swapping to a different metaphor – to be humble is not to be like a balloon that's deflating, whizzing around the room making the same rasping sound that the body makes as it releases gas, and then eventually coming to rest, shrivelled and impotent on the floor. I can't think of a better picture to describe grovelling. My issue with grovelling is that it's still an attempt, whether intended or not, to draw attention to ourselves.

You may have met people like this; they may not go around literally wearing sackcloth and ashes, but their demeanour is one of negativity and gloom[10]. They're the kind of people who can't accept compliments, which I can sometimes understand, but they also fail to give compliments. Their humility leads them to be insular and withdrawn, but true humility shouldn't lead us that way, it should lead us towards a life of generosity and community.

True humility leads us to recognise our gifting and to be generous with that gifting, acknowledging that the gift is itself a gift from God. On the other side, humility identifies its own weaknesses and failings and leads us to be gracefully receptive of the gifts and inputs of others.

Our lives are not to be a statement of how unworthy we are, but a declaration of how worthy He is and of the worth we've found in Him. After all, if we speak of ourselves badly, like we're just junk, then what does that also say of Him? The joy of the Shepherd, as He flings us over His shoulder, should infect our life – He's joyful about finding us, so we should be joy-full at being found.

It's His delight, His movements that flavour our expression.

After Paul writes that we have nothing to boast about, he goes on to also remind the church that they are 'God's Masterpiece'. We might not be the product of our own efforts, but that doesn't mean we're trash either. We are creations that God wants to display; works that speak of His ability, and skill; art that speaks of the Artisan, not of itself.

We need to remember that God is a redeemer, someone who has purchased with the intent to restore those things that He places value on. God values this creation, He loves it, He says it is good, very good – and you and I are a part of that.

Humility then is not about us becoming less than human, but more human. We are not called to devalue ourselves, or others, as garbage or sub-creation. But we are invited to enter into the *renewed* creation that He has redeemed, allowing the old contents of our self-inflated lives to be exchanged for the new helium of His grace and Spirit.

THE HUMBLE, SPIT-COVERED, KING

Jesus was humble. I would even go as far as to say that Jesus was the most humble person to ever walk the planet. And yet He was neither self-centred nor self-destructive, but self-giving.

The Apostle Paul writes in his letter to the church in Philippi, as an example of the attitude we should adopt, that, *'Even though [Jesus] was God, he didn't demand or cling to his rights as God. He made himself nothing, he took the humble position of a slave and appeared in human flesh. And in human form he obediently humbled himself even further by dying a criminal's death on a cross'*[11]. Picture that:

God, the one outside of everything, the source of everything, becoming nothing.

God, the most unrestricted entity that exists, becoming a slave.

God, the source of all that is good, undeservedly dying a criminal's death on a cross.

This is God, giving the fullness of Himself to the whole of creation. From the crib to the cross, Jesus empties Himself, laying down His power, never demanding His rights, refusing to pull rank.

This is God laying low. Emmanuel, God with us. Disguised, and yet fully disclosed, in human flesh.

Marva J. Dawn, when describing the humility of the incarnation, helping us to remember the apparent absurdity of it, puts it as such:

> 'Christmas is not a cute baby in a cozy stable, but the
> harsh reality that God, the Creator of the whole universe,
> so condescended as to give us his Son as a creature in flesh.
> Imagine if a shoemaker would become a shoe'[12]

I don't know how much this will impact you, but I need you to know that Jesus wasn't bling. A man with such resources could have really put on a show! But He's not ostentatious, He's not about glamour. He doesn't use His glory or His power to manipulate, coerce or bedazzle people into following Him. I've got to admit, if I had the powers of God, I think I'd be more like *Bruce Almighty* than Jesus Christ!

Yet Jesus doesn't use right-handed, strong-armed methods of power – forcefully dominating people through violence or buying their allegiance by giving them whatever they want. He's left-handed in His approach. Serving. Loving. Compassionate. Discrete. Inviting others to participate in His Kingdom.

He's not a man empty of purpose and passion, so He's not someone who allows Himself to be walked over – pulled by everyone else's whim – but He doesn't trample over people to get what He wants either.

Jesus leaves himself wide open to be embraced, or to be rejected.

Of course we all need humility when people do love us, when the crowds begin to gather, when people celebrate us and flatter us – we need it to keep ourselves grounded and to discern when we're being used. But it takes a lot more humility to allow yourself to be rejected, without retaliating or threatening to get even[13].

And Jesus understood what it was to be rejected.

Rejected to such an extent, that Jesus permits a fake crown of thorns to be pushed on His head. He allows Himself to be mocked and beaten as He's draped in the costume of a king. A cross becomes His throne, with His royal title also nailed with His body, just above His head. There's no recognition of His status in this inscription – the placard speaks of His crime – the whole scene is one of forsakenness. Instead of being received and welcomed as 'King of kings', instead of being anointed with oil to mark His status, He's spat out and spat at.

Spit. It's worse than scum.

Forgive me here, as I feel we really need to see this scene, but I'm conscious that this might not be to everyone's taste. Spit's an odd thing. We don't mind having our own spit in our own mouths, but once we've ejected it from our own bodies, few seldom want it back. I can't think of anybody who would be happy to drink their own spit after they've spat it out into a glass. I'm certain we'd all refuse if it was someone else's.

And putting aside our sense of propriety for a moment – but we all spit. It may not be public, but when we do spit, it's rarely to eject the normal white saliva that builds up in our mouths. It's when we're trying to clear our throats, or our chest – drawing up the mucus and phlegm that's gathered there, ready to discharge it. You know what the stuff looks like; yellowish-green in colour, slimy, adhesive. I still have this horrible memory of a group of lads at school filling the hollowed top of a fence post with phlegm, and then trying to drag each other into it. Even though some of it was their own just a few moments prior, none of them wanted it now that it had formed a soup with their friends' contributions (ok, I admit it, I was one of those schoolboys). It's repulsive stuff. We don't want it. And sometimes we've even used the stuff to signify, in a powerfully potent way, our repulsion of others. To borrow some of the philosopher Raymond Tallis' words:

> *'Spitting on someone is the ultimate insult... It has the brutal immediacy of a fist on the face. It is halfway*

between a curse and a blow. But it has a particular sinister aspect. It is a forced intimacy, a little rape: the spat-upon is directly exposed to material drawn from the intimate recesses of another's body... The asymmetry of the one who spits and the one who is spat upon is profound: it plumbs the depth of the power relations between humans to its existential bedrock. Which makes this line in Handel's Messiah – "He hid not His face from shame and spitting" – arresting as well as poignant. The image of the Son of God, with sputum trickling down His sweat-glistening, blood-stained cheek is a shocking confrontation with the mad notion of the Author of the Universe taking on the human condition.'[14]

This was Jesus' anointing. Not of olive oil, but the unwanted, yellowish-green discharge from the throats of the Roman soldiers who beat Him, declaring as they did so, *'Hail! King of the Jews'*[15].

But Jesus doesn't spit back. As Isaiah foresaw: *'I do not rebel or turn away. I give my back to those who beat me and my cheeks to those who pull out my beard. I do not hide from the shame, for they mock me and spit in my face'*[16].

He's forsaken, but only words of acceptance are discharged from His mouth.

Here is God. Humbled. Rejected. Crucified. Loving creation through the outpouring of His life. Here is a man of real passion.

WORLD PEACE

Again, I need to point out here that Jesus wasn't weak, just being pulled into anyone's agenda without thought. Jesus was a single-minded person. He had a will, a mission that He was aiming towards – a mission that brought Him into this conflict, a conflict that couldn't be avoided. I need to say this just to clarify any negative connotations that last passage of text might have placed in our minds. I am *not* suggesting that we willingly place ourselves into situations where we allow ourselves to be abused or afflicted or spat at. That's certainly not humility.

But I need us to see Jesus' attitude within His mission, His suffering, His passion, an attitude that Paul says should be an example to us when it comes to living a life of love expressed through humility.

So stay with me here, because we'll take what appears to be a detour away from our conversation on humility as we talk about passion.

Passion is a product of love. Whenever I think of passion I think of those creative types – artists, musicians, writers – so focused and committed to their work that they seem to block everything else out. They lose themselves within their vision as they work to create things of beauty. I also think about my eldest son, with his obsession with *Lego* and Britain's road systems – this stuff switches him on, so much so that it's hard to turn him back off again.

Passion is this spark that seems to ignite people. Despite some people's opinions, it's not always loud and extrovert and wearing a T-shirt. But it's always focused, committed. It's obsessed and fixated with something. So driven that it will do whatever is required to achieve its purpose.

Whatever it takes.

This is why I also think that passion is potentially dangerous. We can become so passionate, so focused, that we lose our objectivity. Passion can stop being something that manifests beauty and devolve into something monstrous, ugly and destructive. It can become detached from its source and start exhibiting tendencies that are unloving, such as prejudice, persecution and violence.

At first it might start as an irritation we feel towards those who don't share our passion. Eventually evolving towards resentment, and then twisting into a hatred of those who seem to object to our pursuits, leading us to exclude them and their opinions from our environments. It may even lead us to become aggressive towards those who we feel stand in the way of us seeing our goals come to fruition.

Linking back to what was said earlier – you can't label people scum and be apathetic about it.

Passion can be scary.

It's a known fact, but maybe one we don't consider often, that the most violent individuals who have ever lived were extremely passionate. Whether that's dictators of the past, modern nationalistic leaders, terrorists, extremists, religious fanatics... all of them have been zealous people.

Doing *whatever* it takes to achieve their goals.

The frightening thing is that when you strip away all their apparent differences, they all share the same ideology – they all believe that the cause they are fighting for, the regime that they're passionate about, is one that will ultimately make the world a better place to live in!

It may shock you to think of it that way. But few people are willing to die for something they truly believe will lead to a future that is worse than the present they currently possess. These 'zealots' believe that the kingdom they are trying to bring in through their violence and aggression is *The Kingdom*, *The World Order* that will bring about peace. Whether you agree with them or not, they're all trying to save the world.

The Roman Empire, for example, was passionate about world peace. They called it the *Pax Romana* – the peace of Rome. They were fanatical about this peace, spreading it everywhere through their military campaigns, and if you threatened to disturb it, they would kill you. Their kingdom had a symbol for this world peace, a logo that they would plaster along roadsides and hillsides to demonstrate just how serious they were about it – a cross – a weapon, a method of execution. This may sound hypocritical, but has anything really changed since then? Even today, when we talk about world peace, and 'keeping it', although we hide behind the picture of a dove, the real symbols at street level are still those of guns, and bombs, and tanks.

It's also worth noting that some nations, both past and present, even invoke God into their passionate pursuit of a better world order, whether that's the Roman Empire, Christendom, the British Empire, Nazi Germany or even IS – saying that God supports them and their means of achieving of their goal. 'After all,' they may say, 'it's his vision we're passionate about...'

I do believe God is passionate about world peace, about saving the world, but I think His passion looks a whole lot different.

THE PASSION OF THE CHRIST

In the fifteenth chapter of Mark's Gospel, we're given the scene of Jesus standing before the crowds prior to His crucifixion, as the Roman procurator, Pontius Pilate, gives them an ultimatum of who should be set free – Jesus or Barabbas[17].

This scene is full of passion. The crowd that gathers is a fanatical group of people. Many in the crowd are obsessed with the idea of liberty from Rome. They long for revolution. And this doesn't just stem from religious tensions, it is also sociological and political – in the ancient world these ideas were seldom separate from each other – it's a hotchpotch of emotions, history and legacy. This crowd longs for freedom. They long for a better world order. They long for peace, but not the peace that Rome has forced upon them. However, they're still willing to use the same methods as Rome to get it – they're willing to fight to achieve it.

All of this is crucial for understanding the choice they are about to make. And to help them in this important decision, some of the religious leaders are circulating within the crowd (or the mob, as the NLT text translates this impassioned gathering), stirring them up, helping them to make their choice a more unanimous one.

They might have picked Jesus. Only a week prior to these events, some of this same crowd were following Him into Jerusalem, passionately waving palm branches, laying down their robes for Him to ride over and shouting out things like, 'Hosanna to the Son of David!'.

To some of us, the word *Hosanna* sounds like the nice word we use in praise and worship services, another way of saying, 'We love you'. But it literally means, 'Save now'. When the crowd are shouting this they're not thinking about 21st century worship meetings – they're thinking 'Here is the rightful ruler, the true King'. But He can't be King until He's dealt with the foreign, ruling parties. Remember that Messiah that some hoped for, the one who would be a warrior like King David? Their *Hosanna* is laden with the expectation that a revolution is just about to begin. They're thinking war – even though Jesus is giving them an opposite picture by riding a donkey into Jerusalem and not a horse. 'Hosanna!' they cry. 'Save us', they shout. 'Let the war begin', is what they really mean.

But since entering Jerusalem, Jesus hasn't done much in the way of a Holy Crusade. He's spent most of His time in the Temple, and most of His protest doesn't appear to be against the Roman enemy – He seems more concerned with the religious leaders, the Temple worship, and trying to tell people that they have the wrong idea of Kingdom. This 'Son of David' hasn't done much towards getting an army together, or even stirring up hatred about the oppressors – He actually teaches crazy things about loving *them*, and blessing *them*, and 'carrying their equipment for an extra mile'.

From the mob's perspective, there's no fight in this Jesus. He's no commando, He's a compromiser. He's even allowed himself to be captured, telling His closest followers not to raise swords –they've abandoned Him, too. And now He stands there, next to Pontius Pilate, silent, dormant almost. There's no passion to this Jesus, they feel, just weakness.

So the crowd rejects Him.

But Barabbas... now here's a different character altogether. Excuse my artistic licence here, but I imagine Barabbas not silently standing by. I can picture him pulling on his chains, protesting energetically about his imprisonment, spitting at his captors and cursing them in his own language (probably calling them something cruder than scum).

Barabbas is a man who possesses qualities that the crowd admire. Some may wonder why they would choose a crook over Jesus, but Barabbas isn't a common crook or a petty thief – Barabbas is a freedom fighter. He's already been part of an insurrection, an attempted uprising, he's a zealous man whose proof of passion is displayed on his already bloodstained hands. The scary thing is, if you asked Barabbas why he did it, why he murdered someone, his answer would probably be something along the lines of, 'For God and His Kingdom'.

The crowd chooses Barabbas. He meets their definition of what it means to be passionate about world peace.

As a bit of trivia here, though an important piece – some translations tell us that this insurrectionist's full name was 'Jesus Barabbas'. If we remember the story of Jesus' nativity, we'll remember that *Jesus* means 'The LORD saves'. *Barabbas*, incidentally, means 'Son of the Father'.

Can you see the contrast that the writer is putting together in this scene?

It's a contrast highlighting the different ideas about how God will bring about this desired world order, a Kingdom that will bring in peace and salvation. Through the passion of Jesus, we're given an alternative to the passionate violence of Barabbas.

And believe me, Jesus is passionate.

Throughout this whole scene, Jesus' actions clearly portray how passionate He is. Not in a typical way, through being extrovert, shouting, jumping and stirring up the crowd. He stands there silent, refusing to be a part of the circus of violence that is going on around Him. In all the versions of this scene that the Gospel writers give us, it's poignant how few of the words spoken actually belong to God.

God loves the world. God is passionate about the future of every nation, passionate about world peace. God longs, as discussed in the previous chapter, to see His dream for this world live and bear fruit. But unlike the fanatics, He refuses to fight for it. God could come, in all His power and enforce His rule, but that would mean His peace would be an illusion just like the *Pax Romana* – a forced peace isn't peace.

God so loves the world that He gives instead of conquers. He serves, instead of slaying. He heals, instead of inflicting hurt and humiliation. God allows himself to become a victim of our violence in order to show us how ridiculous the idea of saving the world through violence really is.

Some might want to proclaim that God is behind them and in support of their passionate, violent pursuit of peace – but here is God, in flesh, showing us that this simply isn't true. He's not sponsoring the state violence, but suffering under it. Here's God, having a crown of thorns pushed on to His head and being mocked. Here's God being scourged and nailed to a 'symbol of peace'. Here's God, crucified, dying from asphyxiation, looking on as people laugh at Him and gamble for His clothes.

Here's God, being spat out and spat at by humanity. God being treated like scum.

And in the midst of this brutality – brutality done in passion – God doesn't cry out for vengeance, or seek to close the doors of His Kingdom to His murderers, He cries out, *'Father, forgive these people, because they don't know what they are doing'*[18].

Jesus is so passionate, so humble, that He gives His life to the cause, and not someone else's.

LOVE ONE ANOTHER

Churches should be the most passionate communities on the planet. Passionate about Jesus. Passionate about life. Passionate about our world and its future. Passionate about our neighbours. Passionate about our enemies – perceived, or real.

But let's be careful not to lose the source of that passion and become fanatical, divisive and destructive. If our passion causes us to become aggressive, defensive (in the negative sense), argumentative or violent, then we are misunderstanding the dream God has for this world, and how He has acted within history to bring it about.

If our 'passion' causes us to see enemies of the dream, or scum who are unworthy to benefit from that dream, then we've let go of the way of Jesus.

We need humility to accept and to express our world's need for the passionate love of God.

We're empty of self, but full of praise for who He is and what He has done. We reject our ways and we choose to walk in His. After all, we didn't qualify for this Kingdom, He invited us into it – He invites everyone into it.

So love the world. Love it like God loves it. Because real love doesn't express itself through what we'll kill for, or fight for, and exclude people from – but in what we'll live for, serve for, suffer for, and invite people into.

And so I invite you into Jesus. I invite you into the full expression of God's love. I invite you to learn and to stumble and to explore, as I am doing, love's way.

> 'This is real love. It is not that we loved God, but that he loved us and sent his Son as a sacrifice to take away our sins. Dear friends, since God loved us that much, we surely ought to love each other. No one has ever seen God. But if we love each other, God lives in us, and his love has been brought to full expression through us' – 1 John 4:10-12 (NLT)

EPILOGUE: **JUST THE BEGINNING**

'Pure spiritual love is a delusion. Love has
come among us in the flesh. It's with our
bodies that we walk in love's way'
Ben Myers.[1]

A CALL FOR SUBSTANCE OVER SHADOW

There's so much more that could be said. When we did this as a series
in our home church – way back in 2011 – we covered more expressions
than those given in this book. We spent some time turning over other
things such as Solitude, Fellowship, Hospitality, Speech... etc. I'm sure if
we spent the time we could keep going, adding even to those – there
would be no end to the ways of expressing love to one another. But for
me, and for this project, I'm choosing to stop here.

Part of my reason for this is rather selfish – sorry. But I'm tired now.
I've devoted a chunk of my time and energy to writing this, and I'm ready
for a break. It's not that I'm tired of *this*, but I'm just tired of carrying
this. I'm ready to birth it, to put it out there and see what happens, to
see what response it has. I don't naively believe that I've necessarily said
anything that hasn't been said somewhere else before. But I'm kind of
hoping that I've managed to say it in a different way – a way that will
help people like me.

But there's a bigger reason than that for drawing to an end.

I feel as if I've already said enough. What I've written is also a massive challenge to me, and to some extent, I don't want to hear anymore – I feel like there is already so much that I need to implement and straighten out in my own journey. I could keep on talking, but it has to be more than that.

In a famous fable told by Aesop, on a hot day two labourers find themselves working in the dangerous glare of the midday sun. Both of them, in seeking what little shelter there is to hand, begin arguing over the small patch of shadow that has been cast by their donkey. The arguing then begins to get as heated as the day, and the debate suddenly becomes their primary focus, erupting into anger and violence. During this, but unnoticed by the fighters, the donkey walks away to graze somewhere else, leaving the two workers wrestling it out in the full exposure of the sun. The moral of the tale is often summarised as: 'In quarrelling about the shadow we often lose the substance'.

That's my personal worry here. Not that I'll start an argument with myself, but that I'll spend so much focus on the shadow – the writing, the ideas, the metaphors etc. – that I'll neglect the substance. This is a love that really requires my body to express it, not a book.

But even here I need help. Maybe you do too? So I'm thankful to be part of a local church, a local community, a local workplace... where this stuff can be practised and sharpened by others also seeking to follow Jesus. I'm also deeply thankful that God hasn't left us alone in this mission – He has placed His Spirit within us – without whom, we could do nothing.

Which reminds me of a prayer I heard once...

Just after starting this project, I had the joy of meeting with one of the widows in our church family, a wonderful lady called Lynne Whittle. Sadly, a few weeks after our meeting, Lynne passed away. But the prayer she shared with me that day, a prayer she told me that she prayed every morning, has constantly been at the forefront of my mind during this whole project:

'Holy Spirit, help me to really love people today'

I share that prayer. I hope you do too. It's a good place to end our staring at the shadows and a great place to begin working on the substance.

ACKNOWLEDGEMENTS

'*We are the music makers. And we are the dreamers of dreams*' is how the famous poem by Arthur O'Shaughnessy starts – admittedly though, I got that from Gene Wilder's portrayal of *Willy Wonka*.

The *we* is quite important to me though, because this dream wouldn't have come true if it weren't for the involvement of others along the way. Those whose contribution to this work – and into myself – have been greatly appreciated:

To Steph, and our sons Corban and Eaden: Thanks for knowing me and still loving me; you make me come alive. Thanks for letting me take this risk and believing that this was something I was capable of. (As a personal note to Eaden – you'd better take care of those gerbils!)

To my good mate Paul Schofield: Thanks for consistently proving what a friend looks like. We've journeyed together for some time now and through some real stuff, but we've always discovered something of the greatness and faithfulness of our God along the way; so here's to more 'broken windows' and 'emails'? Thanks for reading through this, giving your feedback and encouragement. There have been plenty of times when I've questioned myself doing this, but your words have always been timely – even when you weren't aware of it.

To my friend Leanne Magill: Thanks for taking time out of your studies to read and comment on this; your feedback was excellent and really appreciated. On a personal note; I know sometimes you feel like you struggle in this journey of discipleship, but from where I'm sitting you're doing great.

To Peter Nixon: Your expertise in my native tongue has saved this book from becoming one long hyphenated blob. Thanks for sacrificially giving your time to line-editing this. And thanks to Laura too, for sharing that time and for her encouragement.

I also wish to express my thanks to our church family, Metro Christian Centre, Bury, and to our previous home of Bright Meadows Christian Fellowship – thanks for being church!

To those who gave their endorsement to this work – Victoria, Paul, Jeff and Brian – I am extremely grateful for the generosity of your time and your encouraging words; it was more than I had ever expected. Also, a huge debt of gratitude is owed to Jonathan Martin for the contribution of a foreword; I'm still finding it all very surreal, but I'm humbled and honoured to have your words next to my own.

Thanks to the team at WestBow Press for providing opportunities to unheard of voices like my own. In particular, big thanks to Brijit Schmook for helping me to take that first step, and a huge thank you to Jenn Seiler for all her help and guidance on this learning curve of publishing.

Finally, a special thanks to the Holy Spirit – but also a cry of 'Help!' I've just realised I've written a book, and I have no idea where this will end up leading. So help me not to follow this book; help me to keep following you as you lead us into truth.

ABOUT THE AUTHOR

Tristan Sherwin is a husband to Steph, a father to Corban and Eaden, a friend to some, a teacher to many, and a follower of Christ. Tristan, whilst in full time employment, is a Pastor and teacher at the Metro Christian Centre, Bury, England. A lover of books, music and film.

Tristan longs to see that followers of Christ are released to follow and not enslaved. Equipped and not burdened. Engaged and not silent. His heart is that those who claim they love Christ are empowered to express that love.

END NOTES

FOREWORD

1   Excerpted from *With Open Hands* by Henri J. M. Nouwen, pg.27. Copyright ©1972, 1995, 2005 by Ave Maria Press®, Inc., P.O. Box 428, Notre Dame, IN 46556, www.avemariapress.com. Used with permission of the publisher.

INTRODUCTION: AXIS

1   This quote is generally attributed to William Gladstone (1809-1898). Although, I'm pretty certain that something similar to this was also said by Jimi Hendrix.

2   Just in case you're interested; I'm not saying you should watch the film, but, if you do want to hear the full thing in order to get a sense of how these words are delivered (because they are better when heard and not just read), then the scene itself occurs approximately 1 hr and 44 minutes into the film, *Kill Bill Vol. 2*, by Quentin Tarantino, Miramax, 2004.

3   Although, if you do want look into the Historical Jesus – or even just explore the existence of God – then some good starting points, in my opinion, would be as follow's; *The Reason For God*, Tim Keller, Hodder & Stoughton, An Hachette UK company, 2008; *Mere Christianity*, C.S. Lewis, HarperCollins Publishers, 2001 (originally published 1952); *What we talk about when we talk about God*, Rob Bell, HarperCollins Publishers, 2013; *Jesus Outside the New Testament: An Introduction to the Ancient Evidence*, Robert E. Van Voorst, Wm. B. Eerdmans Publishing Co., 2000; and anything by N.T. Wright (aka Tom Wright).

4   Colossians 2:9 (NLT)

5   Erwin Raphael McManus, *The Artisan Soul: Crafting Your Life into a Work of Art*. Taken from the chapter entitled *Canvas*, p168. © 2014 by Erwin Raphael McManus, HarperOne (HarperCollins Publishers). Courtesy of HarperCollins Publishers.

6   See Mark 12:28-34 for the full story.

7   Mark 12:30-31 (NLT)

8   *Blaze of Glory* by Jon Bon Jovi, from the Soundtrack of the same name for the movie *Young Guns II*, Mercury Records, 1994. The lyrics I'm alluding to appear at the end of the third verse, just before the second chorus.

9   See John 13:34-35, 15:12, 17

10 Brian Zahnd, *Beauty Will Save the World: Rediscovering the Allure & Mystery of Christianity*, Charisma House, 2012.

11 The '*Love is...*' passage is found within 1 Corinthians 13:1-7. Even though I'm not referring to this passage within the book, I do hope that after reading this you'll go back to it and read it in a whole new light.

OBEDIENCE

1   Tullian Tchividjian (@PastorTullian) '*Our surrender doesn't produce God's favor; God's favor produces our surrender*' - 10:54 PM on Sat, Jul 13, 2013 – Twitter. Used by permission of Liberate.org.

2   'A very particular set of skills' is an allusion to the infamous quote delivered by Liam Neeson's character Bryan, in the movie *Taken*, 2008

3   See Matt 16:24-25

4   There may the possibility here that Paul's teaching on 'reaping what you sow' (Galatians 6:7) or maybe even Jesus' 'Golden Rule' (Matt 7:12, Luke 6:31) might be entering our minds. Of course, there is nothing wrong with these principles – if we go around causing trouble we shouldn't expect a life free of trouble; if we eat mountains of fast food and exercise only a little then do we really have the right to be surprised when the doctor gives us our cholesterol results? And of course, if you are generous with your time then people will ultimately open up to be more generous with theirs. But it's important to note that Paul and Jesus are not teaching *Karma* – they're teaching responsibility. Sowing good is no guarantee that life will always be good – after all, we all have people in our lives who busy themselves sowing tares amongst our wheat (allusion to Matt 13: 24-29). And, let's not forget that Jesus Himself lived a good life, a sinless life (1 Peter 2:22-23), but was still gossiped about, threatened, rejected and crucified! We could also mention the story of a chap called Job...

5   John 5:14

6   Colossians 2:6 (NKJV)

7   John 15:4

8   Brennan Manning, *The Relentless Tenderness of Jesus*, published by Revell, a division of Baker Book House Company, March 2009.

9   John 13:3 (NLT)

10   Philippians 2:6-7

11   John 11:25 (NLT)

12   Luke 6:43-45

13   See Ezekiel 11:19-20, 36:26-27, Jeremiah 31:33 and Hebrews 10:11-18.

14   Earl Jabay, *The Kingdom of Self*, Logos International 1974, p.72. Used with permission.

LEARNING

1   Werner Heisenberg, *Physics and Philosophy: The Revolution in Modern Science* (Penguin Classics 2000). Copyright © Werner Heisenberg 1958. Introduction Copyright © Paul Davies 1989. Reproduced by permission of Penguin Books Ltd.

2   I'm not a scientist, let's be clear on that, but this sort of thing does kind of 'float my boat'. If, for some reason, you do want to know more about this principle or the sub-atomic realm, then I would quite happily recommend either of the following books by Professor Brian Greene: *The Elegant Universe*, Random House UK, 1999, and *The Fabric of the Cosmos*, Penguin Books, 2005.

3   *Spider-Man 3*, released by Columbia Pictures & Marvel Studios, 2007. Personally, I thought *Spider-Man 3* was a great film – but feel free to question this.

4   Ecclesiastes 12:12 (NLT)

5   This was correct at the time of writing.

6   See Matthew 22:34-40

7   N.T. Wright, *Creation, Power and Truth: The Gospel in a World of Cultural Confusion*, p87, SPCK 2013. Used by permission.

8   See Matthew 8:23-27. Interestingly, a question that recurs consistently through the gospel texts, not only from the mouths of the disciples, but also from the crowds, religious leaders and powers of the day. 'Who is this Man?' is still a question that remains a hot topic within our own societies two thousand years later.

9   See Luke 5:1-11

10   Luke 5:5 (NLT)

11   Luke 5:8-10 (NLT)

12   Dallas Willard, *The Great Omission*, from Chapter 3 – *Who is Your Teacher?*, Copyright © 2006, 2014 Lion Hudson (UK) and HarperOne (US). © 2006 by Dallas Willard. Used with permission of Lion Hudson plc. Courtesy of HarperCollins Publishers.

13   Erwin Raphael McManus, from his contribution to *The Church in Emerging Culture: Five Perspectives*, Zondervan, Copyright © 2003, General editor Leonard Sweet. Used by permission of Zondervan. www.zondervan.com. All Rights Reserved.

14   This insight came from, *Meet the Rabbis: Rabbinic Thought and the Teachings of Jesus*, Brad H. Young, Chapter 2, Hendrickson Publishers, Inc. 2007. Even though I have connected this word to dancing, this isn't something that Young himself does. Incidentally, although I haven't referred to this book further in this chapter, Chapter 2 of this work provides some great insights into how Jesus may have instructed His disciples, and would be good further reading for studying what learning meant within a first century Jewish context.

15   1 Corinthians 2:16, Philippians 2:13

16   See Isaiah 40:29-31

17   2 Peter 1:2, 2 Peter 3:18

18   James 1:22-24 (NLT)

19   Galatians 5:22-23

20   Quote taken from Roy Hattersley's biography of John Wesley: *John Wesley, A Brand from the Burning*, Chapter 4 *Beauty and Virtue*. Published by Abacus, 2002.

MERCY

1   2013 © Erwin Raphael McManus. An Unstoppable Force; Daring to become the church God had in mind is published by David C Cook. Publisher permission required to reproduce. All Rights Reserved.

2   See Matthew 18:21-35. Scripture taken from THE MESSAGE by Eugene H. Peterson. Copyright © 1993, 1994, 1995 1996, 2000, 2001, 2002. Used by permission of NavPress Publishing Group.

3   If you don't understand what I mean by the 'white cat' reference, then I would encourage you to watch some classic James Bond.

4   Romans 3:22 & 23

5   Hebrews 4:15-16 (NLT)

6   Romans 6:12-13 (NLT)

7   Romans 13:8 (NLT)

8   *Splanchnizomai* definition and use in Matthew 18 taken from *Vine's Expository Dictionary of New Testament Words.* If you try pronouncing it, it's actually a good verbalisation of what the movements of innards probably sounds like!

9   Viktor E. Frankl, *Man's Search For Meaning,* published by Rider, 2008. Copyright © 1959, 1962, 1984, 1992 by Viktor E. Frankl. Reproduced by permission of The Random House Group Ltd (UK), and Beacon Press, Boston.

10   Luke 7:47

11   *Hoverboards* and *Self-drying Jackets* are some of the technology available in the film *Back to the Future: Part 2.*

12 According to the story of Joseph in Genesis, God is able to take what is meant for harm and turn it around for good. (Genesis 50:20).

13 2 Samuel 14:14 (NLT)

14 Being* – in the sense of a process, not some instantaneous quick fix. I'm all for being born-again, but birth signifies the start of a course of growth, development, discovery and maturity. I've been recreated, but I'm also still being renovated.

15 Lamentations 3:22-23 (NLT)

16 From *Pastrix: The Cranky, Beautiful Faith of a Sinner and Saint* by Nadia Bolz-Weber. Copyright © 2012 by Nadia Bolz-Weber. Used by permission of Jericho Books, an imprint of Faith Words/Hachette Book Group USA Inc. Also used by permission of Canterbury Press, UK (entitled, *Cranky, Beautiful Faith: For Irregular (and Regular) People*, 2013).

17 Hebrews 1:1 (NLT)

SERVICE

1 THE DOORS, taken from the track *People are Strange*, from the album *Strange Days*, released 1967 by Elektra. Words and Music by THE DOORS © 1967 (Renewed) DOORS MUSIC CO. Used with permission.

2 If you want to explore this idea further, then there's a song by American singer-songwriter Don Mclean called *Prime Time* which is fantastic food for thought.

3 1 John 4:18 (NLT)

4 Luke 10:27 (NLT), quoting Deuteronomy 6:5 and Leviticus 19:18. (In Matthew 22:34-40 when Jesus is asked the same question in the temple, he replies that the 'the Second is equally important.')

5   The Greek words and their definitions used in this paragraph are taken from *Vine's Expository Dictionary of New Testament Words* – thankfully writing the words doesn't mean I have to be able to pronounce them. I am no expert in Greek – I'm not even a novice – so I am heavily indebted to those who are.

6   I grew up with the Vandross version, but this song was originally performed by Crosby, Stills & Nash.

7   See Judges 12

8   To learn more about the extraordinary work of *Hope for Justice* visit www. hopeforjustice.org.

9   Galatians 6:2-3 (NLT)

10   John 1:14 (NLT)

11   Matthew 25: 37-39, 44 (NLT)

12   It might be worth clarifying here that we shouldn't confuse 'serving God' with 'loving God'; one flows from the other. Although, if I'm honest, I do struggle to separate the two from each other – maybe they shouldn't be? John Eldredge's words from his book *Beautiful Outlaw* (Hodder & Stoughton, an Hachette UK company, 2011. Copyright © 2011 John Eldredge) may help us here:

'...doing things for God is not the same thing as loving God... That's like a friend who washes your car and cleans your house but never goes anywhere with you – never comes to dinner, never wants to take a walk. But they're a 'faithful' friend. Though you never talk.'*

This is also a good reminder for our relationships with people too – should our loving them just stop at doing things for them? * Reproduced by permission of Hodder and Stoughton Limited

13   Reprinted with the permission of The Free Press, a Division of Simon and Schuster, Inc. from *The Language of God: A Scientist Presents Evidence for Belief* by Francis S. Collins. Copyright © 2006 by Francis S. Collins. All rights reserved.

14   See Philippians 2:5-11

WORSHIP

1   A.W. Tozer, *The Pursuit of God*, Christian Publications, Inc. 1982. Used with permission of Moody Publishers.

2   See Genesis 9:1-17

3   Genesis 1:27 (NLT)

4   For some more insights on 'the image of God' I would happily recommend the digest of thoughts contained in *Genesis for Everyone* by John Goldingay, Genesis 1:26 (*Friday Lunchtime*) & Genesis 1:27-30 (*Friday Afternoon*), SPCK Publishing, 2010. For a more extensive discussion, one that I came across just prior to publishing this book, see the chapter entitled, *Ecology and the Earth* (section headed *Our earth: divine gift and human responsibility*) within *Old Testament Ethics for the People of God* by Christopher J. H. Wright, Inter-Varsity Press, 2009 edition.

5   2 Corinthians 3:18

6   It's interesting that directly following the prohibition against idols in Exodus 20:4-6 & Deuteronomy 5:8-11 is the commandment about misusing God's name – maybe these two shouldn't be separated?

7   Our solar system actually has two points that we orbit about. One focal point is due to our gravitational attraction to the mass of our sun, the other is caused by our attraction to the remaining mass of the universe outside our solar system. Therefore, instead of having a circular orbit about our sun, it's actually slightly elliptical.

8   Just to be clear, I'm not against expressing God through art, or music, or dance, and at a push, maybe even tambourines – those creative acts themselves are expressions that speak of a creative God, but the responsibility doesn't rest with whatever is created to flesh out the divine. Our own worship shouldn't be so silent, by comparison, that the inanimate becomes more expressive than us (i.e. we should be more vocal than rocks, Luke 19:40).

9   Actually, none of us are, but as Paul writes, our lives can be the things that communicate God's unfathomable favour, unconditional love and transformational mercy. See Ephesians 1:7 for example.

10 See Matt 22:15-22, Mark 12:13-17, Luke 20:20-26

11 I'm not going to go into that here, as I lack the space and talent to be able to, plus it would pull us away from the point I am trying to make. But the scene is worth exploring further, so I would encourage you to read *Jesus and the Victory of God* by N.T. Wright (SPCK Publishing, 1996), in particular the chapter entitled *Jesus and Israel: the meaning of Messiahship*, pp. 502-507).

12 Matthew 18:20 (NLT)

13 The term *'community of professional lovers'* comes from a great bit of writing by Brennan Manning in the chapter entitled *Giving* (pg.125), within *The Furious Longing of God*, published by David C. Cook, 2009.

14 John 4:19-23 (NLT)

15 Colossians 3:17 (NLT)

16 1 Chronicles 21:24 (NLT) (also see 2 Samuel 24:18-25)

17 *The Problem with Pain* by C.S. Lewis © copyright CS Lewis Pte Ltd 1940. Quote taken from the HarperCollins Publishers 2002 edition. Used by permission.

18 A.J. Jacobs, extracted from the entry for *Day 204* of *The Year of Living Biblically: One Man's Humble Quest to Follow the Bible as Literally as Possible*. Copyright © 2007 A.J. Jacobs. Reprinted by permission of The Random House Group Ltd, and Simon & Schuster, Inc.

19 Genesis 1:29

20 Colossians 1:15-20 (NLT) – I would encourage you to read the whole passage.

21 N.T. Wright, *Luke for Everyone*, taken from his commentary of the scene in the temple in Luke 20:20-26, SPCK Publishing, 2001. Used by permission.

22 Sometime after finishing this chapter I read Brian Zahnd's *Beauty Will Save the World*. I suppose that if you wanted to explore this life of worship further, then the beautiful life would be a positive next step in that direction, and the captivating beauty that Brian describes in his book is one that I would encourage you to delve into.

SABBATH

1 Stephanie Sherwin, on Thursday morning 22nd April 2010.

2 Matthew 11:28 (NLT)

3 Here's a test, for you and for myself, and it might be a stupid test, but it's only two questions:

Tell me what your dream is, what you hope to accomplish?

Tell me what the Gospel is (without including your dream).

Which were you most passionate about?

4 Exodus 20:8, Deuteronomy 5:12

5   Walter Brueggemann, *Sabbath as Resistance: Saying NO to the CULTURE OF NOW*, Westminster John Knox Press, 2014. I am deeply indebted to a lot of the ideas that shaped this passage from this excellent book – seriously, give it a read!

6   Exodus 20:11b, Deuteronomy 5:15b (NLT)

7   Luke 12:23 (NLT)

8   As Endnote 5 of this chapter, taken from the Preface, pg xiv.

9   *Ibid*, Chapter 3 – *Resistance to Coercion*, pg 45.

10 Abraham Joshua Heschel, *The Sabbath*, Farrar, Straus and Giroux, 1951. Reprinted with permission of Professor Susannah Heschel, Executor of the Estate of Abraham Joshua Heschel.

11 See – http://www.bbc.co.uk/news/health-29116354

12 As note 9.

13 Thomas à Kempis, *The Imitation of Christ*, translated by Aloysius Croft and Harold Bolton, Dover Thrift Edition, 2003. Used by permission.

14 John 5:17 (NLT)

15 In Luke's gospel alone, see the accounts mentioned in Luke 4:31-41, 6:1-11, 13:10-17, 14:1-6.

16 Philippians 2:12-13 (NKJV) – italics mine.

17 Sarah Bessey, *Jesus Feminist: God's Radical Notion that Women are People too*, Darton, Longman and Todd Ltd, UK. Reprinted with the permission of Howard Books, a Division of Simon & Schuster, Inc. Copyright © Sarah Bessey.

18 Timothy Keller (@timkellernyc, twitter.com) tweeted at 5:05 pm on Mon, Sep 08, 2014. Used with permission by Redeemer Presbyterian Church.

19 The term *'the fad of the land'*, is borrowed from the title of a *Newsboys* song. It's a clever little track. And can be found on their *Thrive* album, 2002, Sparrow Records.

PRAYER

1   Quote taken from *Come be My Light*, by Brian Kolodiejchuk, MC, Rider Publishing (a Random House Group Company), 2008. The writings of Mother Teresa of Calcutta © by the Mother Teresa Center, exclusive licensee throughout the world of the Missionaries of Charity for the works of Mother Teresa. Used with Permission.

2   I can still remember a cartoon that occurs in one of the episodes – there's a little boy pretending to be a Native American Indian; he's wearing a headdress and doing a war dance, when he's joined by another little boy. So he stops his game and turns to greet the newcomer saying something like, 'How! Me um red Indian' (in a stereotypical accent based on cowboy movies). To which the newcomer replies in a typical American accent, 'Indians don't talk like that!'

'How would you know?' responds the actor.

'Because, I'm an Indian!'

It's the ability to get such a powerful idea like that across to a child in such a vivid way that I can still remember it all these years later, which makes *Sesame Street* legendary. Am I the only one who feels that this show should still be allowed to air every day, even if it's the re-runs? #BringBackSesameStreet

3   I should state here, just for the record, that Kermit wasn't my favourite – I'm limiting this selection just to *Sesame Street* alone. If we expanded that context to include the rest of the Henson universe, like *Fraggle Rock* and *The Muppet Show*, then without doubt, Gonzo would be the champion of champions!

4   John 14:6

5   Matthew 6:7 (NLT)

6   See Matthew 27:46; Mark15:34; Luke 23:34, 46; John 11:40-42. You could also ask whether or not Jesus' prayer in Matthew 11:25-27 and Luke 10:21-22 were also audible to the listeners nearby. (Could we include the prayers at Gethsemane and John 17 here as well?)

7   A few paragraphs after these words, Jesus gives us teaching encouraging us to keep asking and seeking (Matt 7:7-11; Luke 11:9-10) – Jesus even told parables to get the point across (Luke 11:5-11; 18:1-8)

8   This might need some explanation as to what a *Truffle Shuffle* actually is – I could provide you with that, but I won't. Instead, I'd encourage you to grab some snacks, invite some friends over and watch Steven Spielberg's *The Goonies*.

9   Isaiah 55:8-9

10 One of the poets of the Old Testament understood this when they wrote '*Because* he bends down and listens, I will pray as long as I have breath!' (Psalm 116:2) [Italics mine]

11 If you wanted an example of this, then Matthew 14:6-12/Mark 6:17-29 would be a good one. To get an audience (and a favour) from King Herod, Herodias' daughter *performs* a dance just for the *opportunity* to make a request of the king – a request that ended up with John the Baptist's head on a platter. This seemed to be the thinking of those ancient societies when it came to approaching those with power – you would come with gifts and repetitive exultations – all in an attempt to be heard and to have your wishes granted.

Again, Jesus' words challenge this tyrannical picture of God by replacing it with a more accurate description – one that better suits the relationship that existed in the Garden of Eden, and not the etiquette of humanity's throne rooms.

But not just Jesus' words; in both passages above (which deal with how earthly Kings heard and handled people's needs), both Gospel writers place the feeding of the five thousand directly afterwards – there's a stark contrast being made between the two. Jesus (God in Flesh), didn't demand the people to perform for Him before doing something – they had nothing to give in the first place. And actually, the people didn't even make the request. Jesus feels compassion and so heals and teaches, and then goes on to provide them with a banquet.

12   Brennan Manning, *The Relentless Tenderness of Jesus*, Published by Revell, a division of Baker Book House Company, March 2009.

13   Taken from *Prayer: Does it Make Any Difference* by Philip Yancey Copyright © 2006 by Philip Yancey. Reproduced by permission of Hodder and Stoughton Limited, and Used by permission of Zondervan. www.zondervan.com. All Rights Reserved. By the way, this is an excellent book on prayer – one of those that I am certain covers a lot of the questions we all carry. So if you want to quit on this chapter and pick up this book instead, you have my every blessing to do so.

14   See N.T. Wright, *The New Testament and the People of God*, SPCK Publishing, 1992. Chapter entitled *Knowledge: Problems and Varieties*, p45; *'To know is to be... ... not merely to observe from a distance'.*

15   Richard Foster, *A Celebration of Discipline*, Hodder & Stoughton, 1989. Copyright © 1980 Richard J. Foster. Reproduced by permission of Hodder and Stoughton Limited.

16   Mark 6:5 (NLT)

17   Matthew 6:10

18   Luke 11:1-13 (NLT)

HUMILITY

1   Gandalf the Grey in Chapter 2 of *The Lord of the Rings: The Fellowship of the Ring* © Fourth Age limited 1954, 1955 & 1966 by J.R.R. Tolkien. Copyright © renewed 1982 by Christopher R. Tolkien, Michael H.R. Tolkien, John F.R. Tolkien and Priscilla M.A.R. Tolkien. Copyright © renewed 1993 by Christopher R. Tolkien, John F.R. Tolkien and Priscilla M.A.R. Tolkien. Reprinted by permission of HarperCollins Publishers Ltd (for the UK and Commonwealth). Reprinted by permission of Houghton Mifflin Harcourt Publishing Company (for the US, its dependencies and territories and the Philippines). All Rights Reserved.

2   Luke 5:27-32 (NLT)

3   Matthew 5:3 (NLT)

4   For the *Prodigal Son*, see Luke 15:11-32. For the *Story of the Great Feast*, see Matthew 22:1-14. With regards to the latter of these parables, scholar J. Dominic Crossan makes an interesting point about the challenge that the open commensality of this feast would have presented about the Kingdom – see John Dominic Crossan, *The Historical Jesus: The Life of a Mediterranean Jewish Peasant*, HarperCollins Publishers, 1992, p262 (paperback edition).

5   Another parable comes to mind here, in Matthew 20:1-16, *The Story of the Vineyard Workers*. In the story an owner of an estate goes, early in the morning, to hire some labourers from the market square. He then goes back a further two times, at nine and at noon, and hires more workers. Of course, anyone hearing this would assume that the owner would be hiring the physically healthy people, those who would have the most to offer. However, on his final visit (at five o'clock), he notices some people still standing around, unemployed, and enquires as to why they aren't working. Their response says a lot, 'No one wanted us!' In other words, no one saw any value in these people. They had nothing to give. Maybe some of them are seen as too weak, too old, too lame... they are the rejects, unworthy of hire. If, like me, you were always the last to be picked for a team in sports (sometimes I was even offered to the other team, 'You can have him') then

you'll get how this feels. But the vineyard owner hires them, despite there being just one hour of working left. The real shock comes at the end of the day, when the wages are dealt out – everyone gets the same amount. Those hired at daybreak get the same pay as those hired at dusk! This, of course, isn't taken well by those who have grafted hard all day. They're insulted, even though they got a full day's wage. It's important to see that the root of this 'felt injustice' is a pride issue – they feel that they have been hired based on their merit, and that their pay is earned in relation to their effort. But what they fail to grasp is that they have only been paid and hired *because* of the generosity of the master. 'Should you be angry because I am kind?' I wonder how many of those 'insulted' workers were happy to work in those fields the following day?

6   See Luke 15:1-7 (also Matthew 18:12-14)

7   Ephesians 2:8-9 (NLT)

8   1 Peter 1:19

9   I owe this insight into privatives to *The Science of Discworld* by Terry Pratchett, Ian Stewart & Jack Cohen, Ebury Press, 2013.

10   Please understand that I am speaking strictly into the context of humility here. I am not talking about those who are genuinely lamenting, or those who suffer from depression.

11   Philippians 2:5-8 (NLT)

12   Marva J. Dawn, *The Unnecessary Pastor: Rediscovering the Call*, Wm. B. Eerdmans Publishing Co, 2000.

13   1 Peter 2:23

14   Raymond Tallis, *The Kingdom of Infinite Space: A Fantastical Journey around your Head*, Atlantic Books, 2009, pgs 20-21. Used by permission.

15   Matthew 27:27-31 (NLT)

16   Isaiah 50:6 (NLT)

17   Mark 15:1-20

18   Luke 23:34 (NLT)

EPILOGUE: JUST THE BEGINNING

1   Ben Myers (@FaithTheology, twitter.com) tweeted at 11:14 PM on Fri, Jan 10, 2014. Taken from his excellent #canonfodder series, this one being his summary of 2 John (my other personal favourite of his was Romans). Used by permission.